Labrador

GETTING ALONG IN THE BIG LAND!

Best Wishes for
Great Journeys!
Winston Whit.

National Library of Canada Cataloguing in Publication

White, Winston C., 1941-
Labrador: Getting Along in the Big Land! / by Winston White
Includes bibliographical references.
ISBN 1-894463-38-2
1. Labrador (N.L.) 2. Labrador (N.L.) -- Description and travel.
1. Title
FC2193.4.W48 2003   971.8'2   C2003-905485-3

The author gratefully acknowledges support of the Newfoundland and Labrador Arts Council.

PRINTED IN CANADA BY FRIESENS CORPORATION

— FLANKER PRESS LTD. —
P.O. Box 2522, Station C
St. John's, NL, Canada, A1C 6K1
Toll Free: 1-866-739-4420 Telephone: (709) 739-4477
Facsimile: (709) 739-4420 E-mail: info@flankerpress.com
www.flankerpress.com

Labrador

GETTING ALONG IN THE BIG LAND!

By Winston C. White

Flanker Press Ltd.
St. John's, NL
2003

Foreword

Nain, Labrador, NL.

September 2, 2003

For many years, all kinds of travellers and adventurers have been coming to Labrador. Some of those who came to live and work here have written good accounts of their life experiences. Others who came as adventurers, tourists or workers have also recorded their experiences. Many of the accounts are rare or difficult to find.

You may be curious as to why I have written this guide to working, living or just visiting our awesome land. Every now and then over the past twenty years or so, invariably someone would remark that they wished they had more information on what to expect or prepare for when they arrive in this great territory. With that in mind, I decided to put together a little guide book. It started with the intention of a small booklet of about 15 to 20 pages, but when I got going, I had trouble stopping. Realizing that there is so much more to add and also realizing the rapid changes that take place as one writes something like this, it seems best to have an option of updating this work with other editions in the future.

My experience of travel is like many local-born people of my generation who strapped on their snowshoes, lashed up their "komatiks" or sledges and harnessed their Labrador Husky dogs, pulled on the oars to paddle the "punt," sculled or sailed small boats, took the coastal steamer from one place to another or stepped aboard different types of aircraft. The information and tips in this guide come not just from my experiences but from many other Labrador men and women, many of whom are living today and others who have left us with accounts of their great and challenging experiences.

Although some of the events described here are horrific or have sad endings, my hope is that these will not deter people from coming to experience and enjoy the beauty this Big Land has in store. This is intended to help you as a visitor to this land, whether you are a construction worker, tourist, a professional or even one of our own residents. My hope is that it will enhance and add to the other travel information already available in print and other forms. I hope it will help make your stay a safe, enjoyable and memorable treasure in your life.

With best wishes, Winston White.

Table of Contents

Labrador — The "Big Land!"..1

The Original Caretakers 6

Our Flag of Labrador 17

    The Labrador Coat of Arms 21

Getting to Labrador 25

    By Road 26

    By Air 36

    By Boat 41

The Labrador Weather 46

    Delays and Close Calls 49

        The Shapio Lake Incident...49

        Rough Landing – Terrington Basin 52

Transportation and General Costs...55

    Vehicles 55

    Helicopters and Airplanes 58

    Wilderness Stories: The Diary of the One Now Dead 58

    Special Needs Travel 63

Politics and Religion 66

The Curse of the North: Black Flies and Mosquitoes 69

Information Services...73

    Accomodations 74

    Food 78

    Alcohol 80

    Possession of Illegal Drugs 81

    Money and Shopping 81

    Arts and Crafts...82

    Communications 84

    Cameras, Film, Flashlights and Batteries 85

    Mail 86

Hunting and Fishing 87

    The Hubbard Expedition 87

    A Guiding Reflection 93

The Rhythm of the Land 95

Activities in Summer 99

    Canoeing 99

    Kayaking 101

    Exploring, Mountaineering and Hiking 102

        The Fitzhugh Expedition 102

    Walking..105

    Festivals and Events 105

Activities in Winter..109

    Snowmobiling and Dogsledding 109

    Snowshoeing 114

    Winter Carnivals 114

    Silent Dangers - Avalanches 116

Perils in Cold Weather..122

    The Saunders and Ford Story..125

    Another Vicious Storm..128

Travel Overland and by Sea 130

    A Cross-country Adventure 130

Camp Stoves, Tents, Food and Water..................................132

Sharing Space with Other Creatures 135

    Small Animals 135

    Wolverines..136

    Wolves 136

    Moose and Caribou..138

    Bears 139

        Bluff the Bear..140

        A Bear Avoided 141

        Moses and the Polar Bear 142

    Birds 143

Clothing and Camping 145

Summary 149

Suggested Reading 151

Images of Labrador 152

ONE

Labrador – "The Big Land!"

Sitting between Hudson Strait and the Gulf of St. Lawrence, Labrador covers nearly 300,000 square kilometres of spectacular scenery. In the north is found Arctic tundra, or the Barren Lands as many of the local residents call it. But barren is just a word applied to an area where there are no trees. In many respects it is a misnomer. Everyone who has had the treat of striding across some of this area and seen the myriad of flowers blooming in our brief summer, or been startled by a nesting ptarmigan, or seen the magnificent king caribou, agrees that the land is by no means barren. The awesome Torngat Mountains, the Kiglaipait and Kamajet group protect this area from the direct fury of the North Atlantic Ocean and the restless Labrador Sea.

Running at a right-angle to our coast, the Mealy Mountains can be seen from Happy Valley-Goose Bay or Cartwright. Another, smaller range of beautiful land lies between Makkovik and Rigolet – the Benedict Mountains. Inland, northeast of Churchill Falls, we can see the Red Wine Mountains, where a small herd of caribou has become known as the "Red Wine herd." The Torngat and Mealy ranges will someday be national park areas.

South of the Barren Lands lie the inland tundra and taiga plains of string bogs, wetlands, marshes and black spruce forests. The pale green shade of the caribou moss lichen is Labrador's own "lawn" and is the natural blanket of this immense land. Integral to the mixture are the pristine blue waters of sparkling lake and mighty rivers. Seventy-five percent of Labrador is covered in fresh water.

Sandy beaches, rocky outcrops, eskers and boulder-strewn valleys and hillsides are some of the footprints left from the last ice age 10,000 years ago. Nearly a thousand miles, or 1,600 kilometres of coastline is carved into hundreds of beautiful bays and long, deep fjords whose walls tower overhead two and three thousand feet!

Off the outer ring of islands along the coast, gigantic icebergs are grounded on the ocean floor. They are too big to continue their trip south. Here they stay and wait for the sun to melt them down by several hundred thousand tons so that they can float and move on. This is why our Labrador Sea is also called "Iceberg Alley."

Our rocks are among the oldest on earth. In the Nain area, geologists have dated them back to thirteen hundred million years ago, and

With your foot firmly planted on a high ridge the landscape and view unfolds as far as the eye can see.

in the immediate area of the community of Hopedale, the rocks are nearly twice as old...in excess of twenty-five hundred million years!

Characteristic of Labrador is Labradorite, a beautiful stone that displays magnificent shades of greens, blues, orange, bronze, or yellow. The magic of Labradorite is best viewed when you dip the stone in water, and let light rays reflect off thin layers to intensify the colours. I have always been told that the Northern Lights come from Labradorite.

There is an old, true legend that says that Northern Lights were once imprisoned in our rocks. A powerful Inuk shaman wandered over the lights reflecting from the stone and with a mighty blow of his spear he freed the lights. Some of the lights didn't make it out of the stone, which is why we have Labradorite today. Labradorite is thirteen hundred million years old.

Another of our resident rocks, called Ramah chert is around 2,000 million years old. Ramah chert is another marvellous stone. We have

Labradorite quarry at Ten Mile Bay, near Nain. Photo courtesy of Leroy Metcalfe.

used it for thousands of years for arrow and spear tips as well as cutting tools. It is very strong and does not crack easily like other stones. Other native tribes learned about its qualities and chert was traded far beyond the Labrador Peninsula. It has been uncovered as far south as the eastern seaboard of the United States. I once read in *National Geographic* about a surgeon in the USA who has been using a scalpel made of Ramah chert. Under a microscope, the edge of the blade made of Ramah chert is smooth while the cutting edge of today's finest stainless steel is pitted and jagged.

When you hike along our shores or over boulder fields you may see soapstone and serpentine for our artists and carvers to shape, and, like Harry Martin says in a song, "release the spirits locked inside." They are the stones used by ancient and modern-day First Nations peoples of this land.

There's another story that says that the Great Creator made this earth in six days and spent the seventh day tossing rocks at the area

Young people, like Jake White and Matt Thompson, love to dig for clams in our clean beaches and cold salt waters.

where we are today. If that's true, a pretty good job was done for us. Among the rocks we have found iron ore, nickel, graphite, dolomite, and rare earth minerals. There are gemstones like sapphires and pretty soon someone is going to stumble over a diamond or strike gold. Mother Nature keeps them hidden in those valleys, hills and beyond the limit of the eye.

Then there are other industries like hydroelectric power, timber harvesting, fishing, and tourism. In "Iceberg Alley" our offshore crab, shrimp, and scallop resources are a bright hope in a changing fishery. Since the king cod stock of Labrador was wiped away from our shores, we continue to live on sea-run trout and Arctic char. Swimming in our cold, clear ocean waters, these fish provide us with a healthy wild food that entices visitors to come back for more.

Other species like clams, whelks, and mussels lie on a seabed floor above deposits of natural gas. Our storehouse of natural resources and the stunning beauty of this land are attracting other people into our once-remote region. But our greatest resource is our people and all you have to do is ask any person for help or direction. You can be sure you will be treated kindly and in a very friendly manner. You will be safe in this region.

TWO

The Original Caretakers

The Innu (pronounced e-noo) and Inuit (e-noo-weet) made the first human footprints on this land. Inuit were until recent years referred to by white people as Eskimo and Innu have been called Naskaupi and Montagnais Indians. Labrador Inuit speak Inuttut, (pronounced e-noot-tut) their ancestral language. It is also called Inuktitut (pronounced e-noot-tee-tue). Innu speak Innu-eimun* (pronounced e-noo e-moone).

Archaeologists and local people with a good eye are constantly finding signatures of our cultures that date from recent times back to five thousand years or more. It is not absolutely clear which of the two First Nations was the first to arrive in Labrador. It may have been the Innu through traces of people whom archaeologists have designated as Maritime Archaic.

Inuit have also inhabited Labrador for a long time. Small oval sod hut remains that Inuit used as their houses have been unearthed. The dwellings had a floor set about a foot deep with flat stone lower walls. A whalebone and driftwood roof frame was covered with a combination of materials such as whale baleen and sod. Heating and cooking stones were set near the entrance and an elevated sleeping and resting platform was situated at the rear and around part of the sides.

This Innu Man, his wife and two youth arrive from the land at my father's trading post at Voisey's Bay. Dad took this photo in 1930. The man has his gun barrel reeved through his snowshoes. The boy carries the axe and snowshoes and the lady has her snowshoes on the toboggan behind her.

For travel in drifting snow, fog or reduced visibility, Inuit erected Inuksuit. Inuksuit (plural of Inuksuk) are made of stones and some resemble a person standing on the land. The word means "thing that can act in the place of a human being." They have helped save the lives of many hunters and travelling families in bad weather. They showed the way to travellers a long way from home. They showed where food was stored on the land in a cache nearby. The Inuksuk also alerted people of a dangerous place or indicated where a significant thing happened so that people should act respectfully in that area. Sometimes Inuksuit would be placed in a row, which would lead caribou to a place more accessible to the hunters.

Every Inuksuk is a strong connection to the land. It is built on the land, it tells about the land, and is made of the land. Inuksuit built with sighting holes in their middle are used for navigation. Each one points to another one farther along the route. By peeking through the small opening toward the next Inuksuk, a traveller is guided in the correct direction. These large Inuksuit can be seen on the distant

This stone cairn protected stored food from foxes and wolves.

ridge and smaller ones are set up in between so that one can keep in contact with them in severe and blinding snow.

New Inuksuit can be built to mark our presence today but the old ones should never be touched. Every Inuksuk is different and unique. It can be small or large, a single rock put in place, several rocks balanced on each other, flat stones stacked, or boulders placed in a pile. The type of Inuksuk depends on the type of stones available close to the site of building.

Inuit are to be respectful of Inuksuit. There is a traditional law my mother spoke about that forbids damaging or destroying Inuksuit in any way. She said there is an old belief that any one who destroys an Inuksuk would be certain to have his or her life cut shorter.

The Innu used similar piles of stone to serve as markers and as they tended to camp where there were trees they also marked tree-tops. Both cultures lived and gathered food from the land and sea around the islands and bays of this northern land. Innu used and lived on the land where Labrador City and Wabush are today.

Historians and archaeologists claim that Norse people were the first strangers to visit Inuit and Innu people. It is also said that the first Europeans to actually settle in Labrador may have been around the early 1700's. In his book "Labrador Missionary" Rev. Armenius Young recalls that he was told by people in the Rigolet area that the first two Europeans to settle in the Groswater Bay area may have been a Mr. Phippard and Mr. Newhook.

This Inuksuk stands in front of our old homestead at Kauk Harbour, near Nain where my father had one of his two trading posts. His first trading post was established at Voisey's Bay in 1913.

From then on, the occasional servant of the Hudson's Bay Company or of some other trading company stationed in Labrador would decide to stay here and become independent fur traders and businessmen. Other workers married local women and took up trapping and fishing as their livelihood, and by the early 1800's there was a slow but steady increase of Europeans settling along our coast and inland bays. It is from these enterprising and hardworking people came the Labrador trapper who traversed the land and into the far western reaches of the height of land where Churchill Falls, Wabush and Labrador City are located today. Starting as young as twelve or thirteen, these hardy souls went through ice, snow, rain, and winds, venturing up to 500 miles and more from their homes on the coast.

These Labrador trappers turned to the great rivers like the Eagle, Sandhill, Alexis, Pinware, St. Paul, Nascaupi, Grand, Kanairatok, Adlatok, and Kenamau as their highways. From their little homesteads they paddled canoes over the waters of the Ashwanipi, Atakonak, Lac Joseph, Ossokmanuan, Michikamau, Sandgrit, Lobstick and Flour lakes until cold weather froze the waters. Then they transferred their loads to sleds and toboggans and on hand-fashioned snowshoes they trapped valuable furs to sell at trading posts. The animals of the land and the fish provided a source of income on which they supported and raised their families. They were a remarkable breed of men who learned the ways of survival from the Inuit and Innu.

Ancient Inuit tentring at the Iron Strand, near Ryan's Bay, northern Labrador.

With the arrival of a wage economy at the start of the Second World War and the construction of the enormous Goose Bay Air Base, many of these men gave up trapping while others maintained the tradition. By the mid-1970's there were few full-time trappers still making a living but those who had left felt the emptiness of working a wage job. Some went back trapping but most kept themselves from going insane in the nine-to-five world with the memories of the better times of an otherwise very hard way to make a living. You will find these men of rare breed epitomized in the songs and poems of Byron Chaulk, Leslie Pardy, Harry Martin and many other writers and recording artists.

We all used canoes, kayaks, snowshoes, and our trusty dog teams for transportation. Every Labrador family had a number of dogs that faithfully hauled the heavy loads of provision, people, and firewood to keep us alive. This amazing hauling dog is described and looked upon by those who owned and used them as an awesome creature capable of such endurance that it actually boggles the mind. Labradorians today, like Toby Anderson and Hubert Groves of Makkovik, are among our people who last used dog teams during the arrival of the snowmobile.

My father and mother, Richard and Judy Pauline White, like everyone else up to the arrival of the snowmobile, kept and totally relied upon Labrador hauling dogs all their lives. My father once described life in northern Labrador:

> "Perhaps the most important among many duties of the hunter to prepare for a coming winter is the care of his team and equipment, for without his dogs the native is almost helpless. Every driver boasts of the prowess of his team, be it five dogs or a dozen and many are the arguments over the merits of the respective teams. The average team consists of eight dogs and in proportion to its size the dog's hauling power is wonderful. Its endurance is even more so and teams have often covered eighty miles in one continuous run on a spring day of seventeen hours and after a feed and a night's rest made the return journey in the same time.

> "I have driven fifty miles a day for seven successive days, food was scarce and the dogs were on half-rations, and the last two days without any food! Male dogs are preferred for team owing to non-interruption of their work by breeding. Bitches are also the cause of desperate fights among the team dogs contending for their favours. A bitch, however, is often

the best leader and the best team of all is said to be a bitch leader with her own progeny following. The sagacity of some leaders in finding trails in bad weather is marvellous and often the driver owes his safety to the leader when all landmarks are blotted out by a snowstorm."

Through a vast expanse of time we have been the caretakers of this land. Our ancestors turned to the land, the waters, the sea and the ice to ensure our survival. The rivers, lakes and valleys were their highways. Around a thousand years ago Europeans began landing and as they settled they mixed with our ancestors and they also learned from the original caretakers to live off this land and care for it as our original peoples did. These people soon learned to use great craft like the kayak and the canoe, and tools such as the snowshoe, the ulu, and drawknife. They used the leather from seal and caribou skins for all types of applications, as we use ropes and cables today.

They made foods like pemmican and nikkuk (dried meat from caribou, seals or other animals) from which the idea for beef jerky was borrowed. In winter they let the frost preserve their food. American Clarence Birdseye was living and working in Cartwright in the 1920's as a volunteer with the Grenfell Mission. According to Chesley Lethbridge, who was born in the Sandwich Bay area, Mr. Birdseye saw what local people were doing to preserve foods. One was the experimentation of Mr. Lethbridge's grandfather who was attempting to find a way to make fish and meats freeze like nature does in Labrador.

Mr. Birdseye seems to have taken exceptional notice of Mr. Lethbridge's idea and that prompted this American to take this northern technology back to the United States where he became famous for freezing foods. Local people say that it was Mr. Lethbridge's idea that really revolutionized the food development in the twentieth century, but that Birdseye got the credit.

Our ancestors used the furs and leather of animals and birds to protect them from freezing. We still use seal, caribou, fox, wolf, black bear, and polar bear skins for jackets, coats, trousers, and boots. Their clothing was made to protect them from the brutal cold and those ageless designs have been adapted and are used today by military and rescue personnel around the world.

From the time when the European traders came to Labrador in the 1700's, fishing for cod, salmon, and arctic char have been the main species taken on a commercial basis. Those who settled here and married Inuit, and much later Innu, made and maintained their own nets and fishing gear. For three hundred years, cod was taken by the millions, and even billions, of pounds from the shores of Labrador. Thousands of tons of Atlantic salmon and Arctic char (this was called Labrador sea trout until the name Arctic char was brought in to use in the mid-1960's) were sent out in pickled form in wooden barrels. Fisherman can never tell what else might be in a net at times. The late Chesley Flowers of Hopedale, one of the cleverest men I have ever met, in 1972 caught a 15-foot grey shark in his salmon net. The huge animal had become entangled and twisted the entire salmon net around itself, but Chesley had his net secured so well that it didn't break away from its mooring. The crew got the huge creature aboard his trap skiff and brought it into Hopedale.

In 1973, another fishermen, Elias Obed, went to his salmon net outside Nain and noticed it had sunk from unusual weight. At first he thought there might be a seal or large mammal tangled in it. When he and his crew got closer, they saw something they had never ever seen in their lives. It was still alive and badly tangled, and though he couldn't be sure what it was, Elias had no choice but shoot it with his rifle. After great struggling, they got it aboard his boat and brought it into to Nain. There it was determined that it was a leatherback turtle. It was a big fellow and it was thought to be around five-six hundred pounds.

The Nain plant had no use for it, and Elias had no use for it either, so I called my cousin, the late Dr. George Story of Memorial University. He took immediate interest and asked if Elias wouldn't mind donating it to the university. Elias was happy to oblige and I arranged a single Otter on floats to come in and pick it up and it was flown to St. John's where the biology department studied the creature. So whenever I go to haul my nets, I always wonder what I might see sometime. So far, few have managed to catch anything as extraordinary and exotic as these men have.

A tent hand sewn of canvas duck with a small metal wood-burning stove for heat and cooking kept the trapper comfortable in the dead of winter.

In Labrador, there are three Aboriginal organizations: the Labrador Inuit Association with a membership of 5,400; the Innu Nation representing about 2,000; and the Labrador Metis Nation with a total of about 4,000 members. Many Inuit live in Happy Valley-Goose Bay and other communities as well as along the northern coast. Metis people live in Southern Labrador communities and in the Goose Bay area. Innu live in Sheshatshiu and in their beautiful new community of Natuausish.

Alongside us live another 18,000 or so people who have come from Quebec, the island of Newfoundland, other provinces, and from other parts of the world. So you see we have quite a bit of space when you consider that about 29,000 people live in an area of 300,000 square kilometres, or 110,000 square miles. But when you observe the different uses – or abuses – humans put this enormous land through, it seems to shrink alarmingly.

With the arrival of more people or "outsiders" as we call them, come new and different values and lifestyles. While we have many different cultures now, English is the predominant language. In the western region around the mining towns bordering Quebec, there is a lot of French spoken. Along the southern coast everyone speaks English but again around Blanc Sablon you can use French. Inuktitut is spoken by Inuit around Lake Melville area and along the northern coast and Innu speak Innu Emiun. Some people make an effort to learn some words like Air Labrador pilot Romain Butler. Romain greets passengers in their own language and while his Inuktitut might sound like Jean Chretien's English, at least he is making effort to speak a little of the language of the people he serves.

Some words in Inuktitut are "Nakummek" for "Thank You." In Innu we say "Naskummetin" for "Thank You." Theresa Michelin is a Service Representative at the Provincial Airlines/Innu Mikun check-in at the Goose Bay airport. Theresa speaks fluent Innu Emiun and just ask her for a few words and she'll gladly oblige.There are several Inuktitut dictionaries about and the Innu Nation is working on its first full scale dictionary.

Design specifications for the flag of Labrador

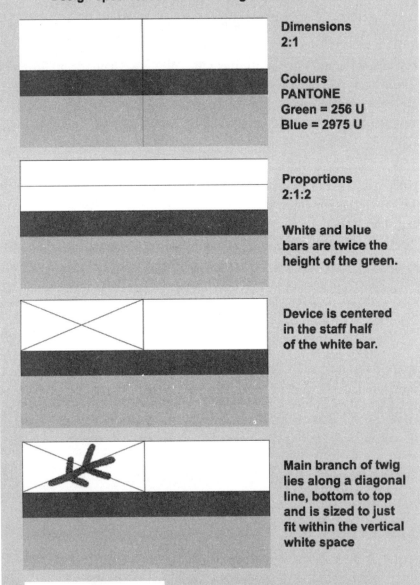

Dimensions
2:1

Colours
PANTONE
Green = 256 U
Blue = 2975 U

Proportions
2:1:2

White and blue bars are twice the height of the green.

Device is centered in the staff half of the white bar.

Main branch of twig lies along a diagonal line, bottom to top and is sized to just fit within the vertical white space

The twig of the Black Spruce tree is in two "year growths" the outer growth being longer than the inner, or earlier, year growth.

THREE

Our Flag of Labrador

When you arrive in Labrador, one of the many things you will notice is the very distinctive flag, flying three colour bars of white, green, and blue. The flag also has a spruce twig located in the outer top white bar. The first Aboriginal Labradorian to be elected to the Newfoundland and Labrador Government House of Assembly was Michael S. Martin. Mike, as many of us fondly know him, is one of the original designers of this great flag.

He told me the story and kindly sent me a copy of his record of how the flag was designed and introduced.

It all started in 1974 when the Government of Newfoundland held a 25th anniversary celebration of Confederation with Canada. The government invited anyone to create a project to mark the event. Mike and his wife, Pat, thought the occasion would provide a great opportunity to celebrate Labrador's heritage.

"We decided that since the province was flying the colonialist flag of Britain we needed a flag of our own. Since the government was not interested in creating a new provincial flag we thought it appropriate to make a flag for Labrador," Mike recalled.

"I set to work on a design and after many attempts we arrived at a prototype that seemed to satisfy the ad-hoc committee that acted as my advisory group. We needed colours that represented elements of our land and an emblem that represented all parts of the country and all ethnic races. The final outcome was a tricolour – white, green, blue in horizontal bars, and in the top staff corner a stylized twig of the black spruce, the tree that is found in all parts of the country and had played a central role in our lives and history," he explained.

The intention was that the flag would simply be a celebration project and the group expected nothing further to come of it. They went out and bought the material in the three colours. "My wife, Patricia, sewed sixty-four flags: one for each town and village in Labrador, one to be presented to each of the three Members of the House of Assembly in formal ceremony, and two for ourselves. I took a felt marker and drew the twig on the white staff half of the flag," Mike continued.

The flags were sent to the communities with letters asking everyone to raise them on March 31, 1974 to commemorate our becoming Canadians on April 1, 1949. At a public ceremony in the main foyer of Confederation Building three flags were intended for the Labrador Members of the House of Assembly. Presentations were made to Mel Woodward, Liberal, Labrador North; and Mike Martin, the New Labrador Party member for Labrador South. The member for Labrador West was Joe Rousseau, a Progressive Conservative, who was also a cabinet minister. Mr. Rousseau declined the invitation, as he believed it would embarrass his government and party.

A month or so later Mike was in Happy Valley-Goose Bay where he called together a group of interested people. He proposed that they form a group whose prime purpose would be the preservation of Labrador's heritage. The Labrador Heritage Society was formed. The Society subsequently formally adopted the flag as the unofficial flag of Labrador.

Our Labrador flag flies as a silent snowman stands guard.

Meanwhile, the attractive flag raised public interest and people were asking where they might buy them to fly on their own properties. Mike approached Herb Brett, owner of the "Mini Mall" to sell them. The flags immediately sold out, and within months there were Labrador Flags flying all throughout the land.

In time, the souvenir trade got into the action. Items such as lapel pins, badges and car stickers hit the market. Many of the images did not conform to the original design. The colours were wrong and the horizontal bars became of equal width and the twig in some instances looked more like the marijuana plant. By now Mike was out of politics and was the Town Manager at Labrador City.

"I proposed to the Height of Land Branch of the Labrador Heritage Society that we apply for copyright of the design in order to try to impose some discipline on the production of these items. The Society was subsequently given copyright to the Flag of Labrador. Unfortunately this had the opposite effect to what we had intended and hoped for. Rather than trying to adhere to the design, distributors of items that carried the flag went out of their way to change the design in the mistaken belief that they could thus avoid copyright restrictions. We had in fact not stated any restrictions and openly encouraged people to use the flag whenever and wherever possible," Mike explained.

"Unfortunately it was these 'bootlegged' images that inevitably found their way onto websites and thus the proliferation of the incorrect version of the Labrador Flag. We find it virtually impossible now to convince anyone that those images are not the original. And no one seems to care much except those of us who had a hand in its creation," Mike noted.

He explains the specifications of the Labrador Flag.

"The overall dimensions of the flag are 1:2. The relative dimensions of the horizontal bars are 2:1:2, that is; the white and blue bars are of equal width and each is twice the width of the centre green bar. The spruce twig is centered diagonally, bottom to top, in the staff half of the top (white) bar, with the stalk closer to the staff and the three branches pointing upward toward the top centre of the flag. This device is sized to take up almost all of the vertical space within the white bar.

"The top white bar of the flag represents the snows, the one element which, more than any other, coloured our culture and dictated our lifestyles. The bottom blue bar represents the waters of our rivers, lakes and oceans. The waters, like the snows of winter, have been our highways and nurtured our fish and wildlife that was our sustenance and the basis of our economy. The centre green bar represents the land – the green and bountiful land, which is the connecting element that unites our three diverse cultures.

"The twig of the black spruce tree, in two year-growths, represents the past and the future. The shorter growth of the inner twigs represents the hard times of the past, while the longer outer twigs speak of our hopes for the future. The twig is typically in three branches and represents here the three original founding races of modern Labrador – the Innu, the Inuit, and the White Settler. The three branches emerging from a common stalk represent the commonality of all humankind regardless of race."

So there you have the story of our flag. It is now widely flown across Labrador and I have spotted it flying on the island of

Newfoundland as well. It is also flown in many places across Canada where Labradorians live and work or where others, who share pride in our history, live. I was quite impressed with the City of St. John's. They have one placed prominently in one of their special rooms in the upper lobby of city hall.

The little flag project has sprouted and grown into a symbol of pride and distinction. The other people who helped in designing the flag were Jack Holwell and his late wife Sarah, Phil Stone, and Cora Poole. These people, along with Mike and Patricia, deserve to be remembered in the Labrador Halls of History.

If you would like to obtain the real, authentic Labrador Flag, contact the Labrador Heritage Society at 709-497-8858 in Northwest River or the Height of Land Branch in Labrador City at 709-944-2209 and ask for Joyce or Ed Montague. They'll help you out.

There are two other flags with similar colours as the Labrador flag. The Innu Nation has a flag and it contains snowshoes and caribou antlers and the Labrador Inuit Association or its Nunatsiavut government will have a flag using the original Labrador flag colours and will have a stylized Inuksuk centered in the flag.

Labrador Coat of Arms

In recent years a "Labrador Coat of Arms" has been produced, using the general themes of our Labrador flag. Like the flag, someone from the Big Land was behind the idea. Wallace McLean, Jr. is from Northwest River and his family roots go back several hundred years to this part of Labrador specifically Kenemesh on the south side in the western end of Lake Melville. Wallace is one of the many people who over the years have advocated the inclusion of "Labrador" to be officially included in the name of our Province. In 2002 the province was officially declared to be "Province of Newfoundland and Labrador." "Wally's" determination to see that Labrador is properly recognized by the provincial government and other people in the province is well known in Labrador and another of his efforts in this respect comes to light with the Labrador Coat of Arms. Wally finished the design of this wonderful coat of arms in 1992. Here is his description.

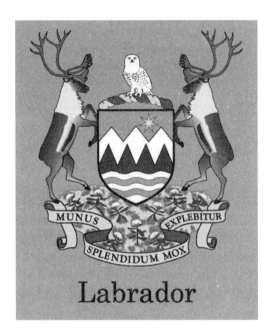

Arms

The primary colours of the arms are those of the Labrador flag: green for the forests, white for the ice and snow, and blue for the waters. The design also evokes the opening line of the Ode to Labrador: "Dear land of mountains, woods and snow."

The three white mountain peaks represent the founding peoples of Labrador: the Innu, the Inuit, and the Settlers.

The four spruce trees symbolize the four points of the compass and the great extent and diversity of the territory, its landscapes, and its communities and ways of life.

The wavy bars symbolize the lakes and rivers, the bays and the sea. The alternation of white and blue represents the changing of the seasons, and by extension, the history of thousands of years of life in Labrador.

The gold star is the Pole Star, symbolic of our northern environment and culture. As a symbol of navigation, it points the way to a bright future. Its points are our grandchildren, for whom we hold the land, its resources, and its heritage in trust.

Supporters

Two caribou, an animal central to the life and livelihood of all Labrador people.

Compartment

A field of Labrador tea and caribou moss.

Crest

A snowy owl (uhu, ukpik) on a gold and red wreath.

Scroll

Red and gold.

Motto

Munus splendidum mox explebitur; "The splendid task will soon be fulfilled."

Adapted and translated from the first stanza of the Ode to Labrador.

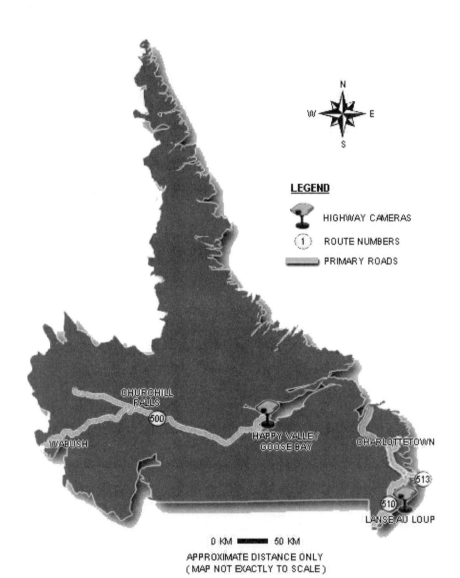

Road map of Labrador.

FOUR

Getting to Labrador

Until as recently as thirty years ago our people were still making full use of the lakes and rivers as roads or highways with which to earn a living and support our families. We used these natural routes to reach destinations where we could hunt, fish, and trap animals in order to survive. Today we still use these natural routes to preserve our traditional lifestyle, to maintain our culture and keep in touch with reality. But now we have a different type of highway. These days a ribbon of gravel road connects us to the rest of Canada and the United States. This road connects Happy Valley-Goose Bay, Churchill Falls and Labrador City and Wabush to Fairmont in Quebec and then south to Baie Comeau and onward.

This route 500/510 connects to route 389 from/to Fairmont in Quebec and then south to Baie Comeau and onward. The distance from Baie Comeau to Labrador City-Wabush is 590 kilometres and takes about 9 hours to drive over the partly paved route. Another 325-kilometre gravel road has been built from Red Bay to Cartwright and this takes about five hours from one end to the other. The "Churchill Freedom Road" was started in 1970 and work carried out on it over a 20-year period in bits and pieces until in the early 1990's the road extended from Churchill Falls westward to Wabush and Labrador City and beyond. The south Labrador road was constructed in the late 1990's and at the turn into 2000.

Many workers from across this Province, including workers from Labrador, built these roads under pretty tough conditions, but our construction people are very capable and can finish the job. People like Barney Power and his crews have done a great job. When more money can be diverted to Labrador we can improve those roads and pave them. The provincial government is going to start paving in 2003/2004 with eight kilometres on one end and seven kilometres on the other end with "chip seal," so it's a tiny start toward a blacktop. But for now, the smoothest ride is in the winter when all potholes are packed with snow and ice and levelled off by Nature.

By Road

If you are approaching Labrador from Quebec City, take Route 138, and 425 kilometres later you will enter Baie Comeau. From Baie Comeau, take Route 389 and head northward for 575 kilometres to end up in Fairmont, Quebec. From Fairmont turn east to Labrador City.

Known as the Churchill Road by many and as the Trans-Labrador Highway by others, route 500 is unpaved and has no services along its route.

The twin towns of Wabush and Labrador City have been mining iron ore since the early 1960's and in 1996 the Carol Project IOCC mine at Labrador City produced the one billionth ton of iron ore since it started mining in 1962. Here you can see the brand new tourism and heritage centre. "The Gateway" project is the brainchild of several Labradorians living in the area who wanted visitors and tourists to get as much information as possible about their area and, at the same time, have a facility in which residents could enjoy local history and culture.

While in these two mining towns, why not take in a tour of the mines? Check with the local tourism office for details. In winter, the world-class cross-country ski trails and the famous Smokey

Labrador's greatest and most awesome wonder is Hamilton Falls, now called Churchill Falls. The falls generated a powerful rumble and the earth underfoot vibrated from the impact of water falling 245 feet into the gorge below. The spray rose in a misty cloud for 500 feet or more and without rain gear, you would be soaked within ten minutes. Here, the author visits the falls in 1962.

Mountain Ski runs offer some of best experiences anywhere. A tour of the huge mining projects with the world's biggest dump trucks is certainly worth the few hours it takes.

There are some dogsled tour operators who can take you out for a silent, steady ride on the land from freeze-up to spring. In summer, the Tamarack Golf course is open, and there are fly-out fishing trips for speckled trout and other sport fishing species. When you are ready to move on eastward to the rest of Labrador, take Route 500, an all-weather, 9.5 metre wide gravel road and drive 560 kilometres to Churchill Falls and Happy Valley-Goose Bay.

If you have the time, stop at Churchill Falls and take a tour of one of the world's greatest engineering projects. You will end up a thousand feet below the earth in solid rock. Churchill Falls was the largest construction project ever undertaken in Canada up to that time (1966), and harnessed hydro power from one of the world's greatest waterfalls. The project was achieved in five short years, with a revolving work force of some 25,000 men and women at the construction site, and countless thousands in manufacturing plants and offices elsewhere in Canada.

The Churchill Falls cataract and river was named Hamilton Falls before Newfoundland Premier Joey Smallwood changed the named to Churchill when Sir Winston Churchill died. Before the falls and the river were named Hamilton, after a British sea captain and explorer, it was known as the Grand Falls and the Grand River. This Labrador giant was among the world's greatest waterfalls and was first seen by the Innu. A Hudson's Bay Company trader by the name of John McLean claims to have been the first European to see the falls. For many years, Labrador trappers stopped to have a look at the mighty waterfall.

Then on August 13, 1891, two Americans, A. Cary and D.N. Cole of the Bowdoin College Labrador Scientific Expedition saw what was then called the Grand Falls. Before they left the falls, Cary and Cole placed a bottle in plain sight and in the bottle they put a piece of paper with their names and the date. The note also suggested that visitors to the falls should leave a similar record. Canadian geologist A.P. Lowe was there on May 14, 1894 and in his note he wrote "285 ft. including drop ¼ mile above." The note does not say which Labrador guides got these men to and from the falls and back to Northwest River on these two expeditions, but there is no doubt they had Labrador guides.

The first mention of guides was on August 11, 1908, when Eugene Delano, Jr. of New York City and Fred Reed of New Brunswick visited the falls, guided by Howard Fineman and Arch Campbell. In 1913, Laurie Coates of Calgary, Alberta wrote "left Grand Village (then Mud Lake) on July 15, 1913 and arrived Fall August 10, 1913. Member of Legion of Frontiersmen. Guide Fred Goudie." In 1915, Arch Goudie of Northwest River placed his name there, and on September 22, 1923, John and Wilfred Groves of Grove's Point in Goose Bay stopped to take in the wonder. Judson Blake (24 years) and John Michelin (20 years) noted on December 10, 1923 that they "came here today from Fred Goudie's tilt on the river. A fine day, can see everything fine. No vapor flying. It's a fine sight." Reggie Blake (21 years) said he was "going down river from Ellis Goudie's trapping place to Northwest River" on December 22, 1923.

There is no doubt that Innu people, including women, had visited this falls long before any of those on the list; however, the first white woman on a list from the bottle appears to be Kate Austen who was there on Christmas Day, 1930 with guide John Michelin and E.P. Merrick. On August 31, 1946 Miss Nora Groves (age 21) and Mr. John Blake (age 29) wrote "traveled here by canoe. Left Mud Lake August 14." On the same date, Barbara Mundy and Russell Groves noted that they "left Northwest River August 14 arrived here August 31. A patch of snow on south side. A beautiful clear day with fluffy white clouds and mist from Falls. Nora Groves and John Blake and 'Flop' came with us. If we ever come again we'll have a look from the south side."

Over the ensuing years, other visitors, like engineers, surveyors, and adventurers came and went. On July 11, 1952, a "party from *LIFE* Magazine, including pilot Marsh Jones (of EPA Gander), guide Henry Blake, photographer Jerry Cook and reporter Leon Jaroff arrived at Grand Falls today. Photographs of the Falls will be published in *LIFE* in October, 1952 as part of a story on Canada. It's a magnificent site and there are no flies or mosquitoes here!"

The outside interest to harness that mighty waterfall to generate electricity had been growing since A.P. Lowe reported on it back in 1894. On May 6, 1954, a short 60 years later, this mighty wonder of the world was further earmarked for development when Edward R. Gilmore and Paul O'Connor of Shawinigan Falls, P.Q., wrote "arrived here at 11 o'clock was dropped in by helicopter pilot Steve Haynes about ½ mile up river. Survey party Edward (Ted) Gilmore and Paul O'Connor to run levels from B.M. at head of Falls to Lookout Lake. Too much soft snow to head across country, will have to follow small creeks and take advantage of lakes. Shawinigan Eng. Co. Ltd. here on Topographical Survey for proposed water diversion and power plant to develop 1,000,000 h.p. Lovely day and a beautiful sight. At present are camped at Lake #16 a good distance from here; hope nothing happens to helicopter. No description of Bench Mark. Looked all over Hell for it, so decided to make trip profitable, descended to foot of Falls and took a lovely picture. Climbed down by the snow slide and prayed to God it would hold. It did which is very evident or would not be adding this note."

From then on activity began to pick up. Beside other names of workers and engineers for Shawinigan Engineering Company and Brinco personnel, Labrador people's names appeared from time to time. Stanley Baikie of Mulligan was there in 1951, Harold Baikie of Northwest River was a guide for three women, Jean Smith, (England,) Myra Miller, (Nfld) Polly Taylor (USA) on June 28, 1954. Gerald Russell from Port Hope Simpson was there on August 15, 1954 and Wilbert Baikie was there on August 21, 1954. Edward Jacque, Abraham Anderson and Herbert Jacque from Makkovik were working for SECO. Edmund de Rothchild of London, England was also there in 1954 and again in 1958. On June 11, 1960 Paul Taschereau and Michael S. Marchant (Mike to many of us who knew him) wrote "this is the final entry in this historic record of visitors to the magnificent Hamilton (Grand) Falls. The original bottle with contents is being delivered to the Hon. J.R. Smallwood, Premier of Newfoundland for safekeeping on behalf of the people of the Province."

In March 1976 the bottle was presented to Joe Goudie, MHA for Nascaupi District in Labrador. Mr. Goudie had it placed in Churchill Falls at the Administration Building of the Churchill Falls Labrador Corporation where it can be seen by visitors.

In 1954, when the Quebec North Shore and Labrador Railway was completed between Sept Iles and Knob Lake (Schefferville today), an opportunity was created for Brinco to extend a 120-mile road eastward from Esker to the Hamilton Falls. The Esker road would allow heavy machinery and equipment to be brought in to the Hamilton Falls project site. Before the Churchill Falls hydroelectric project started there were two other hydro projects completed in Labrador. The first was a two-unit generating plant built by the Iron Ore Company of Canada in the 1950's to supply power to its mine and community at Knob Lake. The second hydroelectric development took place at Twin Falls, when the mighty waters of the Unknown River were harnessed to supply power to the iron ore mines and towns at Carol Lake – later named Labrador City – and Wabush.

Twin Falls, with its five 60,000-horsepower units, generated enough power to light up the two mining towns while at the same time supplying power to Churchill Falls during its construction. And it still had enough power left over to light up all of Labrador. That plant lies in mothball today as much of the water needed to run the plant was re-directed westward to flow through the Gabbro Lake system to help the Churchill generators and turbines. The Brinco group of companies built Twin Falls. The experience gained in that project provided Brinco with valuable experience when it began work at Churchill Falls.

Before you leave Labrador City and Churchill Falls, check to make sure you have a proper spare tire, full fuel tanks and all the basic things you need, as there are no facilities or fill-ups along the road. At present, cell phones don't work along the road and there is no emergency communication system available.

Through the interest of Fred Manson and the Rotarians of Labrador City the idea of getting the provincial government to supply, on a rental basis, a satellite phone to a traveller was put forth. The government now has a system whereby a traveler driving between Labrador City and Happy Valley-Goose Bay or Churchill Falls can obtain a satellite phone for use in case of an emergency. The phone can only be used to call a certain number which will be answered by the Royal Newfoundland and Labrador Constabulary. The phone cannot be used to call any other numbers.

Travellers will make a cash or credit card deposit before getting the phone to cover loss or damage to the unit. The phone will be handed back to a deposit location or hotel on either end of the Trans-Labrador road. Details are available through any hotel, visitor information centre or the Royal Newfoundland and Labrador Constabulary. At the end of the route the phone is returned and made available to the next user.

Use the good old Girl and Boy Scout rule... Be Prepared. This road, especially if it is a rainy summer, can become full of potholes, so be ready for a bumpy ride; in dry weather it is very dusty and like a washboard – drive with care to protect your shock and suspension. During the summer of 2003 and previous summers, even the transport truck drivers were calling on the provincial government for better maintenance of the road.

In late summer 2003, the provincial government announced it would experiment with an alternate type of road surfacing called chip seal on a small portion of the route. Chip seal will be used on eight kilometres of the road from Wabush eastward and seven kilometres will be topped with the chip seal from Happy Valley-Goose Bay westward. There are a good many people in Labrador who don't call it the Trans-Labrador Highway… they say they will call it the Trans-Labrador Road until the day it has blacktop along the entire length of the road.

While you are driving on any of the routes from Baie Comeau onward, beware of the big timber transports. Most drivers find it safest to let them pass and keep a fair distance behind them. You'll still get to where you are going and in one safe piece.

Rare blacktop. Northwest River is now incorrectly called North West River by our federal and provincial governments.

There is another road from Blanc Sablon on the southern Quebec/Labrador border east along the Labrador Straits that will take you through communities like Forteau, L'Anse aux Loup, Pinware and West St. Modest up to Red Bay. 1,500 years ago, Red

Bay was the whaling capital of the world when the Basque Whalers set up their operations there. The archaeological site is a great place to visit and you can see the sunken remains of one of their vessels. From there you can drive to Mary's Harbour, Port Hope Simpson and Charlottetown. On October 31, 2002, the first two trucks drove into Cartwright, setting another milestone in the history of Labrador transportation.

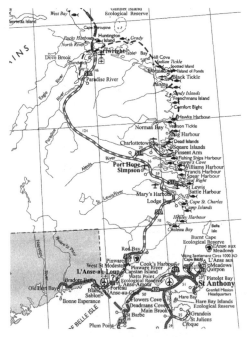

Southern Labrador, showing proposed road from Red Bay to Cartwright.

Again, this is a new gravel road, so you won't find gas stations, air hoses or tire changing equipment between communities. However, the travel time between communities and villages is usually not much more than an hour. It is only one hour from Red Bay to Mary's Harbour where there are two gas stations; 40 minutes from there you are in Port Hope Simpson where there are three gas stations, two along the highway. Another 40 minutes from Port Hope Simpson and you reach the turnoff to Charlottetown (29 kms.) and then an hour

later, you are in Paradise River. You can also drive to St. Lewis and, by the end of 2003, Pinsent's Arm connection will be open. William's Harbour is expected to get a connection in 2004.

Until there is a blacktop or pavement, in dry weather it will be very dusty, and if there is a lot of rain, there will be a good many pot-holes. You should keep your distance behind other vehicles on grav-el roads as small stones can be flicked back at you and if one of those hits your windshield, you may end up with damage. Also consider having a proper full-sized spare tire instead of that miniature thing they call the spare tire that comes with new vehicles today. In winter, parts of this road between Red Bay and Lodge Bay gets plugged with snow so completely that it can take many weeks to become free again, as in some areas it is known to fill in with snow up to 20 feet or more deep! In the winter of 2003/2004, the government is planning to experiment with a winter road around and over the worst places for drifting in to see if that might be a solution to the challenge. The head of the Combined Councils of Labrador, Ford Rumbolt knows first hand about that, so ask for him when you get to Mary's Harbour. He'll fill you in.

You need to be patient, as this is one of the most recent roads built in Canada and our services are not up to scratch as yet. Transport trucks haul freight over this road to and from the ports of Blanc Sablon and Cartwright, so it is wise to take your time and enjoy the scenery. Traffic was up in 2003, as this was the first summer that the road was pushed through. Until more services grow with the demand and people get tourist services up and running, you should bring your own supply of propane and barbecue supplies; however, you can fill up in the Straits and also in Cartwright, so that should not be a problem.

Hotel and accommodations are being beefed up, with Cartwright now increased to 32 rooms, and small hotels in Port Hope Simpson and Mary's Harbour have doubled their capacity. Private accommodations are also being offered. Cell phones don't work in this area, like many parts of Labrador. If you have the extra bucks, a satellite phone would add greatly to your comfort level. Our communities in this region have been there for over 300 years, so you are in for a real treat to experience and share our lifestyle "in the slow lane." I know you will find it most refreshing to meet people who have the time of day to chat and welcome you into their community and homes. So once you're on the trail, don't be shy to ask our local people. As there are few tourism information centres set up as yet, I would suggest you contact the Town Council in any community and you'll find our people most obliging to assist you.

If you wish to experience the sole remaining train ride in the entire province of Newfoundland and Labrador, your only chance is in the Labrador part of the province. The Quebec North Shore and Labrador Railway, also called the QNS&L, rolls out of Sept Ilês, Quebec, up into Labrador City and Wabush in western Labrador. This line was started in the 1950's to transport iron ore from Schefferville (formerly Knob Lake) down to Sept Ilês, or Seven Islands, as Labrador settlers called it. The last spike was nailed down in February 1954. A spur line was built in the early 1960's to link Wabush and Labrador City to the main line. You can spend about eight hours hugging the hillsides of the Moise River and climb up to high land through tunnels and along a maze of lakes and streams.

Once you step down from the train at Labrador City, you can pick up your pre-shipped automobile and take the drive eastward on Route 500, the Trans-Labrador road. Like everything else that you don't have control over, shipping your vehicle ahead can sometimes be a nightmare. I know people who found their vehicle damaged, with missing parts, or vandalized. I know people who drove to Esker – Mile 286 on the line – and when they got there, their car was nowhere to be seen. I know others who found their car damaged and tampered with. It has not happened all the time, but it has happened.

By Air

Now, if you want to leave the car behind and take a plane or a ship ferry you can do that too! Air travel to and from Labrador is frequent but expensive. There are daily flights to and from Montreal, Quebec, Halifax, Nova Scotia Deer Lake, Stephenville, or St. John's, Newfoundland into Wabush Airport or Goose Bay. The national carrier Air Canada Jazz can bring you here and our local airlines like Air Labrador or Provincial Airlines (PAL) will get you safely to and from Labrador.

We like to say in Labrador that we have little to fear when it comes to terrorism but we do hold the unacclaimed distinction of recording the first hijacking of an aircraft in Canada. At Wabush in the fall of 1977, a distraught man ordered a Quebecair BAC 111 jet to take him to Montreal. The crew talked him out of the idea and nobody was hurt.

Wabush also holds the "unofficial" Canadian record, and possibly world record of an unmanned aircraft flight, without remote control. In February 1985, a small, local bush company, Ashuanipi Aviation, had an Aeronca on skis in this western Labrador town. One fine day, the young French Canadian pilot was doing touch-and-go landings on the snow-covered ice of Little Wabush Lake. On his last landing, he throttled back a little too far and his engine stopped. He leapt out of the machine and went over his knees into the deep, white snow.

Now this aircraft required the old, original starting procedure – get out and throw over the propeller a few times until she starts. He grasped the prop and gave it a crank. The engine started and he struggled to get back aboard but as the aeroplane was moving he was knocked onto the snow by a wing strut. To his horror and disbelief the aeroplane took off without him. He had left the throttle at the take-off position! During its first moments the plane narrowly missed the Churchill Falls power distribution terminal, then it flew

Both Air Labrador's Beech 1900 and Provincial Airlines's Saab aircraft carry passengers from major airports into Labrador.

above the community and out of sight over the horizon. The Aeornca crash landed on Gros Ilê in Ashuanipi Lake about 30 miles away. You can draw your own rules to follow if you ever find yourself in this kind of situation. However, have no fear, you are very safe in Labrador, as you will find when you get here. People are friendly, helpful and kind. Remember, its not every day you are going to meet someone who has an aeroplane on skis, that needs a hand cranking to get the engine running!

I mentioned regional airlines like Air Labrador and Provincial Airlines. They serve our two larger airports and from these you can take connecting flights to the coastal airstrips. Today scheduled flights operated by Air Labrador and Provincial Airlines/Innu Mikun go to our coastal communities generally every day of the week except Saturdays. Labrador Airways started the first scheduled flights in February 1976. Captain Ian Massie made the first flight to Nain with a single-engine Otter, landing on the harbour ice in winter, and in the harbour water, on floats, in summer. He was joined by other pilots like Joe Gibbons, Mike Byrne and Tom Simms.

This single engine Otter carried hundreds of passengers and saved many lives over the past 50 years in Labrador.

Under difficult weather conditions and small airstrips, Air Labrador's Twin Otters provide great services to our communities.

By the late 1970's the Labrador Airstrip construction project was underway. This allowed Labrador Airways to secure a twin engine aircraft. They chose the deHavilland Twin Otter. That aircraft model is still in use today. The 19-seat Twin Otter aircraft carries you to the coast but it doesn't have any in-flight service. Like its predecessors, the deHavilland Beaver and Otter, there are no washrooms on the Twin Otter plane, so be sure to freshen up before you get aboard. At the airstrips you'll find local agents who represent the airlines. People like Barbara "Tiny" Andersen, the Air Labrador agent in Makkovik, will always be glad to help you with any question.

The flying time between stops can be from 20 to 90 minutes. Sometimes airsick bags have been used to hold more than an upchuck. There are true stories of big men whimpering softly, trying to hold it, but eventually had to face the embarrassment of walking off the aeroplane in a very awkward manner! Another thing to consider is that the washroom facilities at the airstrip waiting areas along the coast are often "out of order." As for coffee or snacks there are none on the Twin Otters, so consider carrying your own soft drink, fruit, bars or a tea or coffee.

These Twin Otters are extremely reliable aircraft with plenty of power to get in and out of short, unpaved runways, and turbulent and crosswind conditions. Seating on these flights is your own choice but a couple of suggestions here. Avoid sitting near the passenger entrance, especially in winter. If you do sit there, be prepared to see out through the bottom opening of the door. Let other passengers like the hydro or telephone workers take those seats, as they are outfitted and dressed for the extremely cold draught entering that area of the plane. Those doors have been opening and closing for over 25 years so there's bound to be some fresh air. Otherwise, the rest of the aircraft is pretty comfortable and there's ample heat to keep you warm.

This is not the type of aeroplane on which you'll encounter a flight attendant, so ask the crew if you need something. With this in mind, you should wear warm winter boots with dry liners. I have seen many workers, men and women, get on these flights wearing only light walking shoes. I have even seen women in high-heels and nylon stockings at 40 below! Speaking of nylons, I saw a suggestion recently for all women to note. When you travel on an aircraft – or on any form of transport that can have a fire on board – don't wear nylon hose. This material is highly flammable, and when in contact with flame, it sticks, causing extreme burn to the skin and flesh.

Mother Nature controls everything we do in Labrador. Even the flights can be delayed and when you hear the phrase "on weather-hold" it means you can stay put for a while. Often, high winds create unsafe flying conditions, or the crews wait in order to avoid flying in conditions of deadly ice and freezing rain. If you are on a plane and the crew decides to delay takeoff to have the machine de-iced – a process that delays your departure by ten or fifteen minutes, rest assured their decision is for your safety and health.

One older, experienced Labrador pilot once gave me a useful saying for eager passengers with ants in their pants. "If you are delayed or on weather-hold, remember that it's better to arrive late in this world than to arrive early in the next!"

There are several travel agencies in Labrador but the one with the most experience in getting you to and from your destination, especially travel in this remote region is TSI Travel and their toll free number is 1-877-722-7200 and they are also affiliated with the world renown Carlson Wagonlit travel group. Tell them you read about their services in this book.

In your travels you might meet pilots like Mike Bryne, Lester Powell, Kevin Hann, Tracy Squires, Romaine Butler, Glen Cooper and other pilots at Air Labrador. Provincial Airlines has made a business alliance with Innu Nation people and runs Innu Mikun Airlines along the coast. You may have the pleasure of meeting folks like Noel Bennett, whose father Bill Bennett started Gander Aviation, Duane Blake, Trevor Mugford and Ron Lethbridge, all local Labrador boys. The crews on these aircraft are very skilled and work with respect for our weather. They are very competent and have carried many of us to and from our settlements safely. Crews from both airlines have also flown many medical flights to get many of us to hospital and saved countless lives. Sadly, some crewmembers like the late Noel Kennedy and Scott Atkinson and medical staff have lost their lives in trying to save others. There are fitting memorials to these unselfish heroes at the new hospital in Happy Valley-Goose Bay.

By Boat

Marine travel can be just as exciting as flying. Ships and passenger and car ferries run by Coastal Labrador Marine Services can be stormbound by heavy seas or heavy Arctic ice. Between late June and November our coast and the inland port of Goose Bay are served by the Coastal Labrador Marine Services ships *Sir Robert Bond*, *Northern Ranger* and *Apollo* and carry passengers and vehicles. These ships serve the Labrador Straits area as well as the rest of the region. The *Apollo* operates as a ferry between the northern peninsula of Newfoundland and Blanc Sablon. Owned and operated by Mel Woodward and his boys, Peter and Mel Jr., the ferry makes three round trips a day from about May to December and the other two ships operate from June to November. It runs three round trips a day from May to December and the other two ships operate from June to November.

The *Sir Robert Bond* operates between Cartwright and Happy Valley-Goose Bay every two days. This vessel once ran ferry and passengers between Lewisport, Newfoundland and Labrador but since the road link-up to Cartwright, that sailing has been removed. *The Northern Ranger* plys between Goose Bay and Nain carrying passengers, freight and the occasional vehicle is strapped onto the deck.

*The MV **Northern Ranger** carries passengers and freight along our coast.*

Ice and icebergs can delay the start of service by several weeks some years. It has not been uncommon to see a ship arrive at Nain until late July or even early August some years. There have been many shipwrecks and vessels lost to the Labrador Sea. In the fall of 1825, a single big storm wrecked over 25 ships and schooners along our coast and there have been many others over the years.

Icebergs at Hopedale, 1972.

Ice pans float and shift with the winds and tides on our coast.

One of the most recent sinkings was the car and passenger ferry *William Carson* sunk by Labrador ice on June 20, 1977, several hours' steam north of Battle Harbour. It carried about twenty passengers, a crew of about twenty, several cars, trucks, and some heavy earthmoving equipment, and thousands of cases of freshly brewed beer destined for Goose Bay. Labrador received beer in November in those times, and by June, if there were any left, it was getting pretty cloudy and skunky.

The *Carson* steamed into pack ice, and around midnight began to take on water. Fortunately it was a moonlight night and the sea was like glass. The captain ordered the ship to be abandoned and all hands took to the lifeboats, some reaching huge pans where the passengers were able to stand safely until helicopters came out of Gander, Newfoundland, and carried everyone into St. Anthony. The passengers and crew were all well, but everything else went down with the great *Carson* five hours later. So remember, when you get on board any ship or boat, always check out where the life preservers are and where your boat station is. That's the place you have to assemble in case of emergency.

Those are the current ways to get to Labrador but there have been a couple of extraordinary methods used. One chap, Jaromir Wagner from Germany, arrived at Goose Bay from Europe in February, 1980, standing on the outside of an aeroplane. Secured in foot mounts, and a body harness attached to the fuselage, he hung onto the upper wing struts of the aircraft. According to Phil Smith, then a radio reporter with CBC in Goose Bay, Mr. Wagner was pretty cold and numb. Nonetheless, he arrived safely and may have set a world record. A more recent adventurer walked into Labrador from Alaska and others have come in over the Trans-Labrador road on bicycle. I met a chap who drove his 1927 model-T Ford from Texas to Happy Valley-Goose Bay around 1989 or 1990. Another chap was seen coming off the vehicle ramp of the Sir Robert Bond with his knapsack on his back and peddling off into his holiday on one wheel! Never a dull moment in the Big Land!

Local people are a great source of interesting information that you won't find in books. You may hear people refer to Uncle so-and-so. This may not be an uncle of the person speaking at all. In our communities, a person can become "Uncle" to the whole community. For example, if you go to Makkovik, take the time to introduce yourself to Uncle Jim Andersen. Uncle Jim is a walking encyclopedia of history on transportation in our land. You'll leave Makkovik with a wealth of useful and interesting information.

In Sheshatshiu there's the rich Innu culture and people like Greg Penashue, Etienne Andrew, Elizabeth Penashue and Bart Jack are only a few of the people who can walk you through their history. The Mushuau Innu or Barren Land Innu now living in Natuaushish after being settled in Utshimatsits or Davis Inlet since the mid-1960's are the northern relatives of the Sheshatshiu people. Here live people like George Gregoire, Cajetan Rich, David Nui, Katie Rich, William Katshinak, Joachim Nui and Shinish (James) Pastene, just to name a few, who can explain the wonderful ways of the Mushau Innu.

In other communities like Hopedale, Garfield Flowers can tell you yarns that will give you a feel for the life, Abel Leo, Jacko Merkuratsuk or Katie Winters in Nain are just a few among many who can share their history and in southern areas you should try to meet Calvin Poole at St. Lewis, Earle Stone, Frank Clark, Sandy Campbell and the Powell's at Charlottetown, Margaret Burden of Port Hope Simpson and along the way if you get West St. Modeste Agnes Pike is a great source of information. All of these places like William's Harbour, Pinsent's Arm or little Norman's Bay have their local historians who can make your visit to Labrador the full experience it should be.

FIVE

The Labrador Weather

We have a couple of sayings in Labrador that go like this. "If you don't like the weather wait five minutes and it will change" or "The weather changed so fast that we got four seasons in one day!" Well it's quite true that our weather is variable and can change quite rapidly. One early December at Twin Falls on the Unknown River, winter had settled in with the temperature around 40 below Fahrenheit and about three feet of snow on the ground.

The next day it grew mild; the temperature rose to above freezing and snow turned to rain. It rained for three days and all the snow melted down to bare ground. It was about 40 above on the old Fahrenheit scale. Around 8:00 A.M. on the fourth day the temperature began to drop from plus 40°F and by two in the afternoon it was clear and 10 below. By 8:00 P.M. it was -40°F and everything was hard as a rock. That's just one example of how quickly our weather can change.

January is our coldest month. If it hasn't gone south, your thermometer can range from –20 to –30 and better in central and western regions. The coldest I've seen was at Twin Falls in 1963 when we recorded 54 below and without a draft of wind. Another time, in March, 1968 at Twin Falls, I saw lightning and heard thunder. These are unusual, extraordinary and even rare occurrences but nonetheless they do happen.

The Labrador winter can be windy and the prevailing westerly gusts can cut like a razor. Because of local topography, wind directions and speeds can often become violent gusts and storms. Garfield Flowers of Hopedale can tell you many stories about the powerful winds in his area. He was the official weather observer for a dinosaur's span of years. When the United States military was building radar sites along the eastern part of Canada, Labrador was one of the geographic defense regions. The sites contained huge radar domes and antennae measuring several thousand square feet. The US engineers built these structures of the latest and strongest metals and concrete, but two domes and radar antennae were toppled by the winds before engineers redesigned them to withstand the wind forces. This is a land of constant, violent weather changes.

Spring break-up of ice starts with the strengthening sun in April. By late May, the snow and ice inland has turned lakes into flooded reservoirs which begin to spill their way towards the sea. By mid to late June, the interior lands are freed from their icy grip but the lingering pack ice off the coast remains a threat to coastal travel and keeps the temperatures down. Although most snow melts away to feed the streams and wetlands, white snowfields survive some summers and remain in the hillsides for another winter.

Summertime brings a whole range of temperatures. Along our coast it can be cool as our Labrador Sea usually remains at one to three degrees above freezing, and giant icebergs remain grounded and emit a cool draught. In late June, July and August you can experience temperatures between 10°C and 18°C but move inland 40 or 50 miles and you can enjoy temperatures between 20°C and 30°C. Places like Mud Lake, Northwest River and Happy Valley-Goose Bay in the western reaches of Lake Melville often report the highest temperatures in the entire province and sometimes top the Canadian weather charts for a day. Goose Bay has recorded the highest temperature in the province, I believe, at 39°C. When we see a string of hot days in the mid-to-high 20's and 30's the land becomes very dry,

The snowmobile and a boxed wooden sled are used all winter in our Labrador communities.

and the caribou moss can burn like gasoline. Thunder and lightning storms develop and "up-she-goes" with forest fires.

From late May to mid-September, open and camping fires are not permitted and the provincial government bans the use of all outdoor open fires. If you are camping "Labrador style" with a canvas tent and a small stove and stovepipe for comfort on our cool weather days, it is very wise to carry a square foot of metal fly screen to put over the stovepipe to prevent sparks from flying onto the ground around you or even landing on your tent.

Fog is common along the coast, especially in spring and summer when winds blow onshore. The more you move inland the less fog you'll experience but I have seen fog around the Churchill Falls area for several days at a time. On a sunny day fog banks can be seen lurking off the coast and with an easterly or northeasterly wind, the fog will roll in quickly. If hiking or working on the land it is wise to beware of the speed at which fog can come in and reduce visibility to near zero. Prospector Bernard Chaulk recalls having the fog replace an otherwise sunny afternoon in a matter of minutes. He had seen many prospectors caught out in the fog until it cleared hours later or even overnight. As always, it is best to stay where you are, make yourself comfortable and wait until visibility improves or if lost, wait until you are found.

Besides being a good flat expanse for an airport, Goose Bay was chosen as the site of one of the world's best airports because it sees only one to three foggy days a month in summer. We know our weather and how fast it can change and close in and come down in snow, rain or fog. When the wind comes out of the west, we know that the bad weather is going to move out, the sky will turn into that special Labrador shade of blue, and the sun will turn it into a glorious day! I'm not sure who should get the credit for this one, but the first person I heard say it was Greg Baikie, a helicopter pilot from Happy Valley-Goose Bay. It was on one of those glorious days he turned to me and said "Winston, it's a Large, Labrador Day!"

Delays and Close Calls

Travel in Labrador can be easily delayed by bad weather. Allow ample time, preferably a whole day, to make connections between communities. A missed flight in some places can mean a wait for an extra day or two. Boating and camping trips require a few extra days built in to cover the possibility of bad weather. The most common weather factor delaying travel will be wind and, in the case of flying (and sometimes with boat travel), freezing rain or ice. Most times the wind gusts can influence the operation and landing of aircraft.

The Shapio Lake Incident

I have two personal experiences with winds that I associate with teaching me to have great respect for this land. One took place on October 16, 1990. I was on a single-engine Otter landing on floats at Shapio Lake to survey a campsite. There were six of us on board; my wife Debby, my young son Jake who was two at the time, land surveyor Neil Parrott, his technician John Holwell and our pilot Bill Smith.

It was a clear, sunny day and the wind in Goose Bay was out of the west, around 30 to 40 miles an hour. About an hour later we reached Shapio Lake. The wind was high and the lake had about two-and-a-half to three- feet-high swells. After carefully circling the landing area, Pilot Smith touched down and made a safe and naturally bumpy landing, considering the swells. He increased power to turn the aircraft toward shore but it seemed not to respond to his controls. He looked down to his port side and saw the problem. The front three feet of the float had cracked off on impact with a swell and we were unable to turn. He called on all of us to put on our life vests and he called a mayday emergency on his radio.

Many aircraft and helicopters operating in the region at the time picked up the distress call immediately. The broken float on the Otter began filling with water very rapidly and within five minutes the port wingtip was in water and the flight deck and cockpit were partly submerged.

We were also in deep water but the wind was carrying us toward shore. Before we were about to sink, we reached shallow water, the port wing tip touched bottom, and the starboard float kept us afloat. We were in a nose-down, tail-up attitude in the water with the port wing in water and the starboard wing skyward at about 30 degrees.

My wife and Bill had no choice but to vacate the cockpit and took positions standing on the starboard float, holding onto the wing strut. Pilot Smith smashed a cabin window, which Debby could put her arm through to hold on with. Neil Parrot was also on the float, holding onto the float rudder while John remained in the tail of the plane near the door. Captain Smith advised us that no one must leave the aircraft unless he said so and we all agreed. I crouched in the doorway with little Jake huddled between my knees, one arm around him and one arm on the doorframe. I was ready to take him with me if or when the pilot ordered us to leave the aircraft.

At this point a Twin Otter circled over us. It was a comforting sight to see it even though it could not land as it was on wheels only. Twenty minutes later a Universal helicopter came and hovered over us, then landed on the shore to standby and assist us until a military rescue helicopter arrived from Goose Bay. We waited and clung onto the Otter and kept talking and reassuring each other for what seemed like forever. We also encouraged each other to make moving motions with our feet and arms to keep warm, even though we could not let go our hold or shift locations.

The flying time for aircraft like the Beaver and Otter, with a speed of ninety to a hundred miles an hour, from Goose Bay to Shapio is around an hour and ten to an hour and twenty minutes. We clung on to the Otter for almost three hours before the rescue helicopter arrived from Goose Bay and hovered over us. A rescue technician dressed in floatation gear jumped from the chopper and swam toward us with what looked like a floating suitcase. He handed Bill a rope and told him to tug on it firmly. Instantly, a circular raft appeared and one by one we stepped off the Otter into the safety of the raft. With the rescue technician on board with us, the wind carried us to shore where both helicopters waited to take us to Hopedale, sixty-five miles to the nearest nursing station and clinic for medical assessment. We were all fine but some hypothermia had begun to take place. It was only in the days and months to follow that the reality of just how close we were to losing our lives came over us.

CF-NLA fuselage after sinking mishap at Shapio Lake.

Fortunately, the deHavilland Otter is made for the Canadian north and has been used in Labrador since its introduction in the late 1950's. The Otter and Beaver are well-built planes with strong wings and solid airframes. It was this great wing and airframe that withstood the wind and wave action in our situation. Had it been another type of aircraft the story could have been different.

Captain Bill Smith was excellent and kept assuring us that we would be okay. I know he felt a deep personal regret and responsibility for the event, but we also learned later that the metal in the port float might have been fatigued or even cracked as he and other crew had reported excessive leaking just days prior to this flight. As it was nearing the end of the float-operating season, the operator decided to complete this flight and then take the plane out of service during freeze-up. CF-NLA never made it out of the water. A crew was taken in to try and refloat the craft and bring it to shore, but further damage took place and it was later removed in pieces.

Rough Landing – Terrington Basin

My other experience was on a flight in mid-September 1978, coming out of Nain, again on floats. The late Captain Harold Oake was chief pilot and Jim Burton was his first officer. Just after liftoff from Nain harbour into a strong northerly wind, a powerful downdraft or wind shear suddenly slammed the Twin Otter back onto the whitecaps. In a split second, Captain Oake instinctively chose between heading for the beach and continuing his takeoff, even though the aircraft had struck the waves very hard.

The only people on board were a young boy from Goose Bay who had flown up for the ride, and myself, along with two sacks of mail. The crew knew that some damage had occurred involving the struts and cross members between the floats and fuselage. Captain Oake climbed with full power out over the 1200-foot hills surrounding Nain, and was on a southward course when Jim came back into the cabin and told us we had some slight damage and would be flying directly to Goose Bay. He also said we would be climbing to around

9,500 feet in search of the least turbulence to avoid any further jolts on the float and strut system. This turned out to be one of the smoothest flights and fastest from Nain to Goose Bay. I believe it was something like fifty-nine minutes.

When we circled Otter Creek, a part of Terrington Basin where float planes land in Goose Bay, I could see fire trucks and rescue boats on standby for our landing. Captain Oake eased CF-DQY onto the water as one float made contact, and then the other. As everything appeared to take the pressure of the landing, he kept full power until we neared the beach and dock. We tied up without incident and that evening the Twin Otter was lifted out of the water and the cracked and broken spars and struts replaced. This was another smooth and safe landing.

I have often overheard some guys make a remark like "Boy, that was a rough landing!" or "What kind of a pilot was that at the controls!" Another saying we hold dearly in Labrador and one I can say from experience is, "Any landing you walk away from is a good landing!"

Goose Bay Airport's runways are among the longest in North America.

Provincial Airlines Innu Mikun Twin Otter at Nain Airstrip.

My first travel in an aeroplane was in 1954 when I was 13 years old. It was in a single-engine plane known as a Norseman. It was on wooden skis and the entire plane's fuselage and wings was covered with cloth fabric, not metal like today. My next flight was also on a Norseman, in summer when the landing gear was changed over to floats. There were no airstrips or airports in Labrador then. The only place with an airport was Goose Bay. Another experience was in a Beaver, which was a metal aeroplane, still with one engine, and then a couple of years later I flew in a much bigger single-engine aircraft called the Otter. I also flew in Cessna 180 and 185's on skis and floats many times with pilots like Peter Jensen, Gord Reezak and Don Bennett who flew for the Brinco companies out of Twin Falls and Churchill Falls.

Over the years I have had great flying experiences with others like Pilots Bill Eaton, Walter Brown, Clayton Hutchings, Ray Taylor, Len Byl, Ralph Blake, Ralph Bradley, Murdoch Mayo, Hector Baikie, Clayton Pilgrim, Brent Chaulk and Benny Powell. The list can go on an on so I'll have to stop and list those others in the next edition. With wonderful people like these all you need to bring is a relaxed and flexible attitude and you should have the time of your life!

SIX

Transportation
and General Costs

Due to its distance and isolation from major commercial centres, the cost of living is higher in Labrador. Remoteness is the guardian of the pristine areas of the region and to get to inaccessible places you'll find that you pay more. Outfitters and guides are available but you should take care to obtain the services of a reputable and reliable guide. Your life can depend on the skill of your guide if you run into bad weather or other hazards. The cost of air travel is very high due to several factors including the type of aircraft that can be used safely on the 600-metre 2,000 -foot) long, gravel topped airstrips. Fuel in the north is another direct cost factor the traveller has to absorb. Operating in extreme cold temperatures also drives up the cost.

Vehicles

You can rent automobiles at Labrador City, Wabush, Goose Bay and the Straits areas. In some communities, a few individuals may have a car or vehicle for you to use for a few hours. In the larger centres, however, the leasing companies make you agree not to use the rented vehicle on the Trans-Labrador Road (Churchill Road as it is called in Happy Valley-Goose Bay), or on other gravel roads in and around the towns. Some of the smaller communities have a taxi service from the airstrips into the town, like East End Taxi in Nain. Some hotels like the Atsanik Lodge in Nain have Tom Goodwin or Sara Webb to pick you up. Woody Lethbridge and his son Dwight at the Cartwright Hotel in Cartwright provide transportation to and from your flight and are available to take you around the town.

Cartwright Hotel is one of the many small but comfortable lodgings along our coast.

Labrador people have many skills like building boats most suitable for travel in our waters.

This craft, we call a flat, shows the clever craftsmanship that many of our people developed to meet their needs. Working with few sophisticated tools, they produced dependable, yet inventive vessels.

All the smaller communities are compact enough to be explored on foot but there are many ATVs and snowmobiles. ATVs – or Four Wheelers as we call them – are common during summer and fall, but once there's enough snow down, out come the snowmobiles. Don't be surprised to see a whole family heading off to school or to the store on a single machine. It's the way we get around in our communities.

If you are interested to take a boat adventure, ask around the community for a reliable boat owner and operator to hire for a few hours and explore around some of the bay and islands. Most of the boats are made from new materials like fiberglass but you will still see many homebuilt boats. These vessels are handcrafted and the skill is handed down through time. The skill of the craftsworker can be seen in the lines and flow of the hull. This industry is still kept alive through fellows like Tony Coish in Happy Valley-Goose Bay, Ford Walsh and Selby Mesher, who are among a few who are still building boats.

Helicopters and Airplanes

We use airplanes and choppers far less than we did twenty years ago because there are now more road links. However, we still need aviation to reach good hunting and fishing places not accessible by road or snowmobile. There are still bush planes available for charter out of Wabush or Goose Bay. There are two helicopter charter companies in Goose Bay and along the coast there are a couple of small operators like Labrador Travel Air out of Charlottetown in southern Labrador. When you travel on these great aircraft you should check with the crew as to where the emergency location equipment, emergency rations, life jackets and other essential items are stored on the aeroplane.

Wilderness Stories: The Diary of the One Now Dead

There have been some stories with very sad endings and others with good endings. Many sad events took place during WWII over Labrador, as Goose Bay airbase was a major destination. One such story comes from a typewritten diary entitled The Diary of One Now Dead. The diary had been circulating for many years and was given to me in the mid-1970's by Nelson Sherren in Wabush. The typewritten note with the diary said the author was unknown. In 1978 I was working as a radio broadcaster at CBC in Goose Bay. I decided to turn the diary into a radio story for Remembrance Day. I felt the people in the story deserved recognition in some way for their bravery in the fall of 1943. To my amazement, I found in my investigation and research that the writer was Grover C. Hodge. This information had hitherto been unknown by many of the people who had copies of the diary.

This sad story starts when a group of airplanes, which had been delayed in Greenland for several days due to bad weather, finally takes off for Goose Bay, Labrador. As they approach the Labrador coast, the planes lose sight of and contact with each other. One of the planes, a B24, breaks out of the cloud and finds itself alone. The crew calculates that they are south of Goose Bay so they turn northward. After some time they realize that they are too far northward and low on fuel. They make radio calls but receive no reply. It is now dark and the engines sputter for gas but there is none. The captain has no choice but to bring the aircraft down. In the darkness he lands safely in a small valley with rocky terrain; there is no injury to his crew of seven, or to the aircraft, which remained mostly intact. They take star shots and estimate that they are about a hundred miles north of Goose Bay. They bed down for the night in hopes of reaching Goose Bay by radio in the morning.

Radio contact is impossible despite attempts, which include putting up an antenna made of rifles and wire. After a couple of days, two members, one of them the sergeant, decide to try and make it south to Goose Bay by water. They are never heard tell of again.

From the third of December, through Christmas and into February the five aircrew remain in the fuselage of the aeroplane, first living on rations, chocolate bars, one bird they caught and ate, and finally only on snow water melted over a small fire made from engine oil. Living on the hope that their two companions had made it south or that they would be found, they slowly starve and die from the freezing cold. At one point in late January they surmise that they might be not too far from a village called Hebron. They are only thirty miles from help.

Two Inuit hunters from Hebron, Joshua Kautjasiak and Joshua Obed, come across the wreckage and remains of the crew in March as they travel overland towards their camp at Ikkigasâtsuk . They abandon their hunting trip and return to Hebron with the news and a larger party goes to the site.

Sam Lyall and Bill Metcalfe explained to me what they found. "The inside of the plane was covered in soot from the fire they kept going from engine oil. Their hands and faces were black from the soot of the oil," said Sam.

"I remember they were all young-looking fellows, It was pitiful," said Bill. "We wrapped them up and put them on the komatik and took the bodies to Hebron."

A military plane was sent from Kuujjuaq, then also known as Fort Chimo, and the remains of Captain Hodge and his crew were taken back to the Ungava Bay base and buried. The remains were later exhumed and moved to Fort Pepperell near St. John's from where they were returned to their hometowns in the USA.

About fifteen years later, the United States decided to build a series of distant early warning bases along the Labrador coast. One site they chose was Saglek; the crash site of Flight Lieutenant Hodge and his crew was just a few hundred yards from the airfield they built. A monument was raised in 1978 to commemorate the ill-fated crew. In 1998, a student at the Robert Leckie School in Goose Bay turned the incident into an excellent play at the Labrador Creative Arts Festival. In 2001, CBC Television Producer Bob Wakeham in St. John's paid a great tribute to the crew and surviving families in a documentary, and in it the American family called on anyone who might know where the original diary might be to contact them.

In relating the story to John Jararuse of Nain, who was born near Hebron, I learned of yet another twist of fate in the sad story. John told me that his parents lived at their little homestead even closer to the crashed soldiers at Pangernatok, only ten miles south of the plane. He added that his father, Martin Jararuse and his brother Jacko went hunting by dog team in early January that year. Their north course for walrus took them along the lower shore below the crash site and they noticed that their dogs picked up a scent of something and attempted to turn up into the hills. The two hunters surmised it to be a scent of land animals and commanded their team to stay on course. The irony is that the dogs could have found the crew and some of them may have been saved as they were still alive at that time! Does the Great Creator make these calls or are they just the hand of fate?

With small aircraft, the unseasoned traveller should be aware of propellers and tail rotors. Ask your pilot about anything on your mind. Chopper pilots like Wayne Massie, Don Simmonds, Bert Barr, Wayne Roberts, John Danby, John Innes or young Zoe Webb from Nain want their passengers to know how to move and work around these wonderful machines.

Workers at the Voisey's Bay project, like Richard White (author's elder son), put safety around helicopters as the top priority when leaving or approaching the machine.

Pilots like these will explain the dos and don'ts of the business. They will tell you to always approach and leave a helicopter from the front and never around the tail. Keep anything like fishing rods, maps cases, or long objects low and preferably horizontal to the ground. There have been some ugly and fatal accidents.

The same caution applies to bush planes. When you are standing on an aircraft float, do not stand or move across the red line marked on the leading bow of the float. This red line marks the path of the propeller. Always wait for the engine and propeller to completely stop before you proceed beyond that line. One lucky fellow I know noticed that his leather jacket had a clean cut across the shoulder blade area, but he didn't know how it got there. He later recollected that he had felt some wind around his neck and shoulder when he was stepping off the float of a Beaver. He spent the next few days shuddering over his close call. The same caution must be taken when you are around Twin Otters and other aircraft. The propeller of any aeroplane is dangerous and you must be always alert.

Jim Burton keeps his deHavilland DHC2 Beaver in top shape.

A flight in a single-engine aeroplane is an experience I highly recommend. On the Beaver, and especially on the Otter, the engine makes a few loud backfires and bangs, but that's just normal. Seasoned users of these planes just casually remark that's the normal sound to expect of the Otter and it wouldn't be right if you didn't hear it. After travelling in a huge jet at 600 miles per hour, it's pretty cool to sit in one of these small aircraft and cruise along at about 90 mph. While many of the original pilots of Eastern Provincial Airways like Ian Massic, Bill Eaton, Clayton Hutchings and Joe

Gibbons have hung up their wings, veteran pilots like Mike Byrne are still around. These names are among the many bush pilots who, with their great skills and knowledge of local flying conditions, saved many lives getting people safely to hospital. Then there are the many technicians and engineers like Gerry Penney, Roy Boyle, George Furey and Steve Chaulk, just to name a few, who kept these machines safe and airworthy. I have always been comfortable in the Beaver or the Otter and if you get the opportunity to take a flight in one of those wonderful airplanes, you will get a very good idea of why I call this 'the Big Land'!

Special Needs Travel

As a general rule, travellers who have special needs should be well prepared in advance when travelling in Labrador. If you need wheelchair access and facilities you will find yourself in situations that can be awkward or difficult. Most of the aircraft have access and interior space for wheelchairs, and crews on the coastal vessels handle the needs of wheelchair travellers well. I have seen a sports fisherman assisted into a Beaver aircraft, his wheelchair folded away, and taken off to a remote lake to enjoy a fishing experience. As they say, where there's a will, there's a way.

Outside the larger centres like Labrador City and Goose Bay, health facilities are limited and special drugs or equipment may not be available. Carry enough medication to cover your stay and allow for unexpected delays. Carry a month's supply for a two-week visit; medication should be carried on your person, not packed in luggage in case this has to be left behind due to load restrictions.

Medical and dental services are available in larger towns in Labrador, but in small communities you'll find a small health centre staffed by a couple of nurses and general staff. If medical needs cannot be met there, the patient is flown out to a larger centre for attention. Doctors visit the smaller communities from time to time but may not be there when an emergency occurs. Should the unexpected

Our nursing stations repond to all kinds of medical emergencies, as well as the daily medical needs of the communities. In this photo, the author's wife, Debby, attends to a cut foot of a young Innu child at the Davis Inlet clinic.

happen and you are for some reason injured or become ill, you may have to be airlifted or "medivaced" to Goose Bay or beyond.

The Health Labrador Corporation operates a Twin Otter air ambulance aircraft between the coastal villages and towns in to Goose Bay or St. Anthony. From the larger centres, the Provincial government of Newfoundland and Labrador runs another air ambulance in a King Air pressurized airplane capable of carrying the sick to larger hospitals in St. John's or Halifax. Like the Twin Otter, a nurse and or a doctor will often travel with you to assist and care for you. Again, very experienced pilots are behind these life saving flights; for many years Ted Piercey was captain on this service and then Glenn Cooper and his father Royal Cooper.

Today, George Furey, Jr., is one of the competent crewmembers piloting this airplane. So that you are prepared, non-resident visitors should check what kind of medical coverage they have and how it will work away from home. It may be wise to purchase supplementary coverage before leaving home.

Generally speaking, visitors to Labrador do not need immunizations other than those needed to get into Canada from other countries. It is a good idea to make sure all your regular immunizations are up-to-date before you come to an isolated region like Labrador. If you are bringing pets you must make sure their shots for rabies are up-to-date, as rabies is quite common among foxes, wolves, and other animals in the region.

Twin Otter and skidoo - You don't see these in New York!

SEVEN

Politics and Religion

Four elected members represent Labrador in the Newfoundland and Labrador House of Assembly. At the time of printing our provincial members of the House of Assembly were Wally Andersen, Liberal, representing the District of Torngat Mountains in the north; Randy Collins, New Democratic Party, representing Menihek district in the western part of Labrador; Ernie McLean, Liberal, representing Lake Melville and Yvonne Jones, Liberal, representing South Labrador. On the federal scene in Ottawa, Lawrence O'Brien represents Labrador in the House of Commons. All five are from Labrador. All representatives have offices in their Labrador districts as well as in the cities where they attend to government business. Over the past couple of hundred years there has been evidence that a number of people living in Labrador always felt they were poorly represented in the Newfoundland government. Labrador was out of sight, out of mind.

Labradorians got fed up with this and the first sign of breaking the tradition of electing a Liberal was in the early 1960's when the district of Labrador West voted in an Independent member in Charlie Devine, who was living in Labrador City at the time. The remaining districts voted in representatives sent in by Premier Joey Smallwood from the island part of the province. A new political party was found-

Protest camp flying Labrador flag during the construction shut down of the Voisey's Bay exploration camp.

ed at Twin Falls and Labrador City in 1968 when Tom Burgess, Morris Chaulk, Max McLean and this writer wrote the framework and mission statement for the Labrador Rights Party. For the next two years the party spread from the west to the east and Goose Bay. There were hundreds of men and women who put their time and energy into the growth, including Malcolm "Mac" Moss and Charlie Jubber. During that most exciting time, Tom Burgess met Mike Martin in St. John's and Mike joined our cause. In 1970, it was decided to change the name and the party became the New Labrador Party (NLP). Tom Burgess left the Liberals and sat as an independent. In 1971, Tom was re-elected as the member for Labrador West and Mike Martin was elected as the member for Labrador South. Melvin Woodward kept the seat of Labrador North for the Liberals. Mike Martin became the first Aboriginal to be elected as a Member of the Newfoundland House of Assembly in history.

The NLP remained active until the late 1970's and faded into the background as the Liberal and Progressive Conservative parties began to select local people to run as candidates. That period was one of the most vibrant and exciting political times in the history of Labrador. Now, in 2003, there is a new call for the New Labrador Party to become active once again.

For your spiritual needs, churches are located in nearly every place except at the Voisey's Bay project site. In the small and older villages and settlements, clergy from the Moravian, Anglican,

United, and Roman Catholic Churches live there or visit every few weeks or so to hold worship services.

There are also some lay preachers. These four religions have been in Labrador for several hundred years, but other churches like Apostolic, Baptist, Jehovah's Witnesses, Pentecostal and Salvation Army have arrived over the past fifty or so years.

This Moravian Church in Nain was built in 1922 after a fire in 1921 destroyed the church built in 1771.

EIGHT

The Curse of the North: Blackflies and Mosquitoes

Labrador, like northern Quebec, northern Ontario and northern Manitoba, is a haven for black flies and mosquitoes. They are around until the frost kills them. Another pesky insect is the deer fly or stout as we call them. These are large, about the size of a bumblebee. They

Mosquitoes and the blackfly will try to nip through anything.

cruise around your head and body and like to bite. You have to be quick to hit these bugs; it takes quite a wallop to actually knock them out of commission. The long beautiful days can be turned into days of frustration and a downright curse by the infestation of swarms of these insects. While the wind is gusty and high it can be quite bearable; however, once the wind drops on a day when it's warm enough for them, they will swarm around you by the millions. It seems that they just love the different brands of repellent, so it's wise to carry a good supply of repellent.

Some people like the spray repellant while others prefer the liquid squirt container. The only advantage of the spray is that you can give your cuffs around wrists and ankles a good covering. I like to carry both. A mosquito hat with a screen is good and the new bug jackets and shirts also help. If you are caught without any of these new products, try some old proven ones. Wrap your head and shoulders in a shawl-type material or wear a large kerchief around your head and ears. Sometimes waving a branch of a tree or a willow around your head is great when you have stopped for a rest. Our people have done this for a long time.

The remains of a 1927 Model "T" Ford sits at the site where US Commander Donald MacMillan abandoned it in 1928, near the Voisey's Bay construction campsite at Anaktalak Bay. This motor car was equipped with skis on the front and tracks on each side at the rear, introducing the first "snowmobile" to residents living in the Nain area.

Back in the early 1980's, I was guide for two chaps from the Provincial Department of Mines who were interested in the old 1927 Ford motorcar left at Anaktalak Bay by US explorer and adventurer Donald B. MacMillan. It was a fine, sunny day with a light breeze over the blue sea as we left my place at Kauk Harbour and headed up the bay. When we reached the site, it was still a glorious day and we began to look over the abandoned car. We were quite enjoying everything when within a minute or two we were surrounded by millions of blackflies, every single one of them looking for a fresh meal. They were so numerous that even though we were standing only three or four feet from each other, all we could see was the outlines of each other through the clouds of mesmerizing blackflies. Both Wayne Tuttle and Wayne Ryder were seasoned travellers in Labrador, but this was the worse blackfly attack they had ever experienced.

My two guests relax and enjoy the peace and scenery at a less blackfly populated beach after their ordeal near the old MacMillan campsite.

We had to cut short our stay, run for the speedboat, get it into deep enough water so as to get the outboard motor running, and then hightail it out of there. As the wind picked up with the speed of the boat, we were able to shake off some of the insects but it took about five minutes at twenty-five miles per hour to rid ourselves of them completely.

Perhaps the best advice is try to prevent them from crawling inside your clothing. Secure the cuffs around your wrists and around your ankles to reduce their chances of further advancement; I find what they call a jac shirt with a hood useful and wear repellent. There are several types of repellents made with trademarks like Muskol and Deep Woods Off which keep them at a distance for a short while before you need to lay on some more. Try to put up with them as best you can and try not to let them "drive you around the bend" as they are very much part of the territory.

Norman Anderson picking rhubarb near Voisey's Bay.

NINE

Information Services

The provincial government of Newfoundland and Labrador operates tourist information booths and offices at Labrador City-Wabush and in Happy Valley-Goose Bay. In Labrador City, there's the brand new

Ed and Joyce Montague in front of "The Gateway" at Labrador City. Ed and Joyce are among the many hardworking members of the Gateway and Labrador Heritage Society in Labrador City-Wabush.

building called "The Gateway," which is operated by the Height of Land Branch of the Labrador Heritage Society. Inside is the history of Western Labrador area beginning 3500 BCE to present day. The exhibits include the prehistoric stone tools of the earliest Innu culture, the French and English fur traders, an earlier 1895 exploration of Geologist A.P. Low and his ill-fated gold rush. This building also holds the Labrador West Tourism department and a craft and souvenir shop operated by the Labrador Heritage Society. People like Andy Spracklin and Edmund Montague (originally from Northwest River) were among many to pursue this idea into reality and the interpretation section of the building is called the "Ed Montague Exhibit Hall."

In these tourism centres you can find printed information from hotels, campsites, bed and breakfast locations, fishing, hunting and touring information. If you are travelling and visiting in the region, you should make a habit of listening to the radio as tourist alerts are broadcast daily. This service is available for you in case there is an urgency or emergency back home and someone may want to reach you. The message usually asks that you contact the closest RCMP or in western Labrador area the Royal Newfoundland/Labrador Constabulary.

Accommodations

I won't list all the hotels, bed and breakfast locations, and camping facilities in Labrador, as you can find these in the tourism information centres, but I'll name a few; perhaps in an updated version of this booklet, we can provide more. Some Labrador town and communities now offer hotel or lodge accommodations. In Wabush and Labrador City there are the Carol Inn, the Two Seasons Hotel and several bed and breakfast operations. There are also other bed and breakfast operators and in every community there are people who open their homes to tourists. East of Wabush is Churchill Falls and the Churchill Falls Inn is a good place to stop and rest. Along our coastline accommodations have improved and grown in the past 20 years. In Nain, there is the Atsanik (means Northern Lights in Inuttut) Lodge. Jessie Ford, a local resident, takes in guests and provides great meals of local foods. Jessie also sells the best homemade bread I've come across and for $3.00 a loaf; you won't be sorry. I arranged for guests from New York City to stay at Jessie's in the summer of 2001. They were so impressed with Jessie's bread that they took several loaves back to their families and friends in the Big Apple.

When you are in the Nain area you will be just on the doorstep of the newest major nickel, copper and cobalt deposit in Canada and the

Project construction, Voisey's Bay camp, Anaktalak Bay.

The brown hillside in this photo of the Voisey's Bay mineral discovery is called the ovoide and will be the site of the first mining activity. The road snakes its way northward to Anaktalak Bay campsite and wharf facilities.

world. The Voisey's Bay mineral deposit and mining project is underway but the project does not have any provision or capacity to accommodate tourists. The only way to get on the site is if you are working there or providing a service to the owners. You may be able to see some of the wharf and shipping facilities as the MV *Northern Ranger* now has Voisey's Bay in its schedule of port stops. Just remember you will not be in Voisey's Bay as you will be in Anaktalak Bay. The camp and shipping facilities are at Anaktalak and when the mineral deposit was discovered in late 1994 it was called the Voisey's Bay discovery. The original Voisey's Bay is about 20 kilometres south of the construction campsite. The Voisey's Bay project is owned by Inco and this company has established a very respectful and meaningful relationship with our Aboriginal people in the area, Inuit and Innu.

For the first time in the history of a major development in Labrador, we see a company working with Aboriginal people to help them train and prepare to work with the company in well-paying jobs and careers. This will no doubt set the tone of other development to

Town Hall, Happy Valley-Goose Bay.

follow in the future, and it is something the people and the company can be very proud of.

If you are going to Hopedale, Eddie and Patty Pottle operate the Amaguk (meaning wolf) Inn. In Makkovik, Randy Edmunds and Laurie Dyson offer all you need at the Adlavik Inn, and just thirty miles or so inland at Postville, Priddle's Lodge is clean and comfortable. Max and Bridgette Blake offer accommodations in Rigolet and you can buy your food from Chew's Take Out or the local Northern Store.

Bradley's B&B in Happy Valley/Goose Bay is on the list of many tourists and business travellers.

In Happy Valley-Goose Bay Linda Green operates Bradley's Bed and Breakfast. Her number is 709-896-8006 and there are a couple of other operators as well. There are four hotels to choose from, including the Labrador Inn, the Royal Inn, the Aurora, and the newest – Hotel North. If you want to experience a more peaceful atmosphere, or have a travel-trailer, try Goose River Lodges about ten kilometres along the Northwest River highway.

Cartwright is the largest community south of Goose Bay. The Cartwright Hotel is a fine establishment and the hospitality is great.

Now that a gravel road is linking communities from Blanc Sablon, Quebec, to Cartwright, you can drop in on any of the small settlements and find accommodations. The Northern Lights Inn in L'Anse Au Clair, Noel Lodging and River Lodge Hotel in Mary's Harbour, Ocean View Resort in West St. Modeste, the Sea View in Forteau, Alexis Hotel in Port Hope Simpson, the Charlottetown Inn in Charlottetown are just a few of the establishments you can duck into at the end of a good day. While you are in Charlottetown, you can charter a plane through Labrador Travel Air, which operates from this community. The plane can take you fishing or almost anywhere you wish.

There are many special sites and places in this exotic land that are not in the glossy brochures, but local people know them. Among the recent sites restored to accommodate visitors is the historic fishing village of Battle Harbour, in southern Labrador. I remember anchoring at this harbour in the 1950's when it was one of the main ports of call on the Labrador coast. The fog was always thick here and the "air was fresh with salt" if you know what I mean. Fishing stores, houses, an inn, and stages have been restored and this is a fine place to visit and enjoy the passing icebergs on their way to Newfoundland.

If you are travelling alone to small communities you may find that you will have to share a room if the space fills up. You should try to make your arrangements in advance, especially in summer as local accommodation often fills up with workers who are in the community for the short summer construction season.

Food

For the most part you can expect standard North American fare like chicken, pork chops and steak. Some of this food has travelled a long distance and may not be as fresh as you are accustomed to. However, Labrador food is hearty and plentiful. Often, local country food is served. Ask for Arctic char, caribou, seal, Arctic hare or ptarmigan. Ptarmigan, a member of the partridge family, is an excellent source of protein and it is low in fat. It contains more iron than store-bought chicken, and is an excellent source of B vitamins. Caribou is very nutritious, rich in protein and iron, and low in fat, so it is a great choice for the diet-conscious.

A small store in Happy Valley-Goose Bay called Uncle Sam's sells fresh-frozen caribou steak, roast cuts and prepared caribou burgers. Most visitors who have tried the caribou burgers never went back to the big yellow arches of the fast food world again.

Seal and Arctic char carry the all-important omega-3 fatty acids, which prevent heart disease and are a great source of vitamin A and B as well as protein and iron. Arctic char is found across the circumpolar world and has been a staple in the diet of Aboriginal people for centuries. It is a member of the salmon family and winters in our lakes and every spring takes to the rivers to spend a couple of months or so in our cold ocean waters. The Torngat Fish Producers Cooperative in Happy Valley-Goose Bay sells fresh-frozen, ice-glazed Arctic Char in whole fish form. Served up as baked, steamed, pan fried or in any of your favorite dishes, the pleasures and benefits of eating this wild natural food has been known by us for many generations.

At the right time of year you may get local favourites like scallops, crab, or shrimp. When in season, tasty and healthy delights like bakeapple jam, red berry (partridgeberry) pies and blueberry pies will tempt your appetite. I've had red berry jam at Cartwright Hotel and it was among the best I've tasted. Ask for it during your stay.

If you get the chance, try some of the older recipes from Labrador. When you walk or drive through our communities, especially on the northern coast, you might be taken aback when you see animal rib cages, or strings of fish fillets hanging outside our houses. Sometimes you will also spot them hanging inside, especially in winter or during poor summer weather. Don't panic. These are 4,000-year-old recipes, time-tested and proven to be most nutritious; they can save you from hunger and starvation under extreme conditions.

Pitsik, dried Arctic char, or any other fish, is very good. Nikkuk is dried meat from caribou or seal. Both delicacies are eaten just as they are because Mother Nature has prepared them with the wind and sun. Some people now add spices when they prepare the food before hanging it to dry.

My wife's friend, Cathy, who is from St. John's, loves Nikkuk and we can't keep it stock when she's around. She stands on the tall side so the Nikkuk is in danger no matter how high we hang it. These foods are part of our culture just like ice cream or candy is part of yours. You may also spot a small type of building that looks like an outhouse, but with smoke rising out of it. Don't panic and call "FIRE!" as it is likely a smokehouse full of Arctic char. Our people use smoking as a way of preserving and putting up fish. After the char is cleaned and split, it is salted either in brine or with loose salt for about one hour. Then the salt is cleaned off and the fish dried slightly to strengthen the skin. Previously collected, dry blackberry (also called crowberry) bushes and sod are added to a small fire in a rotted tree stump, which provides the slow heat. The sod smoulders and the berry bush provides the flavour. Try it. The fantastic taste will blow you away!

Alcohol

In the larger centres local, national and international brands of beer, wine and liquor is on the shelves. The legal drinking age is 19 so save yourself embarrassment and carry an official identification showing proof of age. In the coast communities there is beer available at the local beer store unless the stock has temporarily run out. The communities that have a hotel usually have a licenced bar. Beer is a favorite and if you are going to carry some, we buy the cans so they don't break open (and break your heart) and make for a lighter load than bottles. We also love our rum and coke. You may have good fortune on your side and be invited to a party. Before long the music will come out and the first thing you know, you're the guest at a party around the kitchen table. The long yarns and stories that can be shared over a dozen beer and a bottle of black rum will remain with you forever.

You may find some of us speak fast or with funny accents or sayings. It's all part of our colourful culture and language which remained the same through generations of isolation. People who serve you at the airlines, hotel or restaurant may not call you by name. If we don't know your name or forgot it, we will call you 'my love' or 'my darlin' or 'me b'y' or 'me buddie' until "we gets to remembering your name."

Someone once said that if you don't understand something one person said ask another. If you still don't understand, pretend you did and enjoy the friendship and happy times anyway.

Possession of Illegal Drugs

Possession or sale of opiates, narcotics and hallucinogens is illegal. Possession of illegal drugs is a serious offense and you could find your holiday abruptly suspended. Never carry packages or parcels for someone you do not know well, without verifying the contents. Respect community standards and you should have no problems.

Money and Shopping

Only the larger towns of Happy Valley-Goose Bay, Wabush/Labrador City, Churchill Falls, Blanc Sablon, L'Anse au Loup, Cartwright, and Nain have bank services. Only a few communities outside the larger centres provide automated bankcard service. In some communities, local stores and business operators will cash travellers cheques in Canadian funds, but cash shortages often occur in these places, especially after paydays, so it is a good idea to carry cash in a secure fashion. Some stores and hotels accept credit cards. Herman Webb operates Haynes Store in Nain. He and Enos Baggs at Labrador Investments are very accommodating, and with a phone call, will gladly take care of visitors' needs. It's the same if you are on the southern Labrador at Powell's in Charlottetown, or at Penney's in Port Hope Simpson. From Cape Chidley down to Lanse Au Clair, you'll never be left out in the cold! Outfitters generally accept credit cards, but individual guides accept cash only.

Check the store hours in the community, as many are not open after 6:00 P.M. and some close on Saturday and Sunday. If you require fuel, be sure to fill your tank on Friday as most gas stations on the coast close for the weekend.

Arts and Crafts

There are a few craft and art stores in the communities but sometimes you'll find them closed. Quite often you see artists or their representatives offering carvings or jewellery for sale. The Labrador Friendship Centre on Grenfell Street in Happy Valley-Goose Bay operates the Drumdancer Art and Craft shop where you will find a wide range of authentic, locally, handmade products at very reasonable prices. Bruce Haynes at Northern Lights Store has a fine gallery of Innu, Inuit and local art and carvings, as well as Herb Brown at Birches Gallery. Kathy Davis operates a nice little gift shop at the little mall near the Labrador Inn and in the T&R Building near the Labrador Inn you find two good shops. Artists and craft producers also sell from their homes.

If you need snowshoes, Eric Flynn in Happy Valley-Goose Bay can make up a fine pair to get you sailing across the fields of snow. He uses local birch or juniper for the frames and fills them with new synthetic materials and adds a good harness made of inner tube rubber from huge earth-moving equipment tires. If you wish to experience a different type of craft, try a Labrador sea grass basket or bowl fashioned by the hands of Garmel Rich. Garmel makes the most exquisite, simple and beautiful handmade grass baskets around. She prefers the grass from the wind-blown shores of Bluff Head, her birthplace outside Rigolet in Groswater Bay. If you're looking for something special, yet small, durable, and easy to carry, give her a call. There are other great artists who have been carving and painting for many years and there are new younger artists coming into their own. Ask around and you may hook onto a true Labrador treasure to take home.

Garmel Rich works with special hand-picked "salt water grass" from coastal Labrador to create her amazing and beautiful grass workbaskets.

Another must is to visit *Them Days Magazine* also just off Grenfell Street in Happy Valley-Goose Bay. This magazine was born out of the Labrador Heritage Society in Happy Valley in the early 1970's and a few years after Doris Saunders became its editor and started collecting stories and photographs of Labrador history and culture. She and many other volunteers and contributors have done a great job over the years. Today Pam Andersen is the new editor and continues the important work of the magazine.

There are other art and craft shops and galleries that you will find listed in the community tourism information outlets. In them you will find works from Shiela Harvey, Heather Igloliorte, Gerald Mitchell, Barbara Wood, Joyce Blake, Isobel Watts, Debby White and Yvonne Webber just to mention a few. You may also be fortunate to meet some of our wood and stone carvers like John Terriak and Gilbert Hay in Nain, or Ross Flowers in Hopedale or Abraham Zarpa and David Terriak around Happy Valley-Goose Bay. You can also ask anyone who will gladly help you find artists.

Communications

Labrador is linked to the outside world by satellite, telephone, television and radio. Most business operators and individuals use modern telecommunications like fax machines and computers to communicate with the rest of Canada and around the world. Some still use radiotelephones, but by and large, Labrador is now well equipped with modern technology to link you back to your home.

Telephone service is available in every community, but pay phones are scarce. Visitors not staying at a hotel or lodge that offers telephone service can usually get permission to use a phone in any building that serves the public, or by asking privately. It is wise to carry a calling card number to which you can charge long distance calls. Occasionally, the phone service might fail or be out of service for a short while. Along our coast, the telephone service is provided through a series of towers and antennae perched upon some of the highest points of land. One of these is Monkey Hill, about 3,000 feet above sea level. Up there the tower and equipment is exposed to everything that Mother Nature can lash out, including freezing rain and ice. Technicans have had to go up to towers like this by helicopter and remove ice up to four feet thick from a tower that is only two feet in diameter! It is any wonder that the long distance service is not out more often than it is.

The Canadian Broadcasting Corporation (CBC) transmits television and radio to all communities. Cable TV is widely available and more and more people are using satellite dishes to receive programs. CBC carries radio on FM to all Labrador communities, with programs originating in Goose Bay, St. John's and Toronto. Steele Communications originates radio programs from St. John's and can be heard on 1230 AM. Short-wave radio is also received from around the world including the Voice of America, the BBC and Radio Moscow. If you would like to hear what Innu-eimun (other spellings in other publications: Innu-aimun; Innu-aimu) or Inuttut (Inuktitut) sounds like, you can receive the OkalaKatiget Society broadcasts, and CBC North radio broadcasts from Nain and Iqaluit. Innu-eimun is also broadcast in Sheshatshiu on a small FM station.

Cameras, Film, Flashlights and Batteries

Most supplies can be bought at the main towns but when you get off the beaten path, you can get basic film supplies like 35mm film for prints but slide film or other special types may be hard to find. Digital supplies are limited, as are video supplies. Batteries, particularly special types like those needed for cameras, watches, and digital equipment, are not readily available in the smaller communities, so bring an adequate supply. You can expect to get AA's, C's, 9 volt, and D's but any others will be sometimes unavailable.

As for the latest digital cameras, I've heard quite a few people say what I'm about to alert you about digital cameras. They work well indoors and on warm days outside but at 10, 20, 30 or even 40 below, they just can't cut it. I've seen them fail within five minutes at 20 below, and at 40 below you can't be sure whether you have captured that special scene or shot. Carry your camera under your outer wear and use your old regular manual 35mm workhorse which will be sure to operate under those temperatures.

A flashlight is an all-important piece of equipment to carry around. Hand-held lights are standard, but have you tried the headlamp style? I got one from Santa Claus last Christmas and it's in the bag among my best and most important gear. As special batteries are difficult to get I suggest a headlamp that uses AA or triple A. Tape spare batteries and a spare bulb on your head straps for good measure.

A short word about photography, especially under snow and ice conditions as there will be a lot of glare. In the long, bright summer days sometimes the best photos are taken early in the day or later into the evening. Keep cameras under your outer clothing in winter and make sure they stay dry during boat travel.

Polar Bear in water. Photo by Dave Reddin.

Mail

Don't expect door-to-door mail delivery; all correspondence has to be picked up at the local post office. Mail is flown to the smaller communities so service can be affected by poor weather. If you expect to be in Labrador long enough to receive mail you should have it addressed to the post office you expect to be served by. Have the mail marked "hold for pickup." Community post offices are often attached to a home, so ask around for the location and hours of operation. It is common for the lone postal officer to have to leave to meet a plane or go on a personal errand. The provincial designation from Canada Post has now been changed from NF to NL to take in the official name change in our Province from "Newfoundland" to "Newfoundland and Labrador."

TEN

Hunting and Fishing

Tourists have been coming to Labrador for many years. In the 1700's and 1800's, tourists looking for hunting and fishing experiences visited our coast on ships from St. John's and United States ports. Captain George Cartwright enticed some wealthy hunters to come from England.

The Hubbard Expedition

There were others who came for the adventure. Americans like Leonidas Hubbard and Dillon Wallace came from the east coast of the United States for adventure in 1903. With their Indian guide, George Elson from Ontario, the two Americans attempted to cross the great land from Northwest River to Ungava Bay, but this trip ended in disaster. The trio took the wrong route from Grand Lake and ended up returning from the interior, starved, weakened and discouraged. Too weak to travel farther, Mr. Hubbard sent Dillon Wallace and George Elson on to get help. When they returned they found their friend had died.

A couple of years later, Mr. Hubbard's wife Mina succeeded in finishing the trip across, thus becoming the first "white" woman to make the trek. Of course, many Innu women had made this trip and hundreds of others over their great history of occupancy in Labrador and Ungava.

In 1925 my father, Richard (Dick) White was living in Voisey's Bay and he offered the following vacation in Labrador.

"Northern Labrador, the Magnetic North! Not chiefly a wilderness of ice and snow, but virgin hunting ground, whose Esquimaux, Indians, dog teams, fisheries and healthy, vibrant climate call you to a vacation of health, pleasure and interest. Sportsmen can here meet the primeval in its truest sense and recuperate their energy in the vivifying air and intense silences of the north. It has become a necessity for the big game hunter of the United States to look ever northward for his quarry. Owing to reckless slaughter and other causes, the caribou of Newfoundland are fast following the Beothuk Indians to the happy hunting grounds. Ethnologists will find an interesting field for study in the native Esquimaux and other tribes. We will introduce a party of not less than four, nor more than six blooded sportsmen to a feast fit for the Red Gods. Time covered – July to October.

"Come now, before the Esquimaux and big game of the north join the buffalo and passenger pigeon of American and the great auk and caribou of Newfoundland in the halls of yesterday.

"Fishing – Includes salmon, sea trout (Arctic char) and cod-fish on the coast, and for those who like to penetrate the interior a short distance the famous "namycush" (lake trout) of the Indians, a large game fish worthy of the keenest skill.

"Hunting – Includes seals and porpoises in the bays, black bears, timber wolf, wolverine, caribou, geese, duck of various kinds, ptarmigan, partridge and the Arctic hare.

"The native Esquimaux, alas, fast vanishing, are well worthy of study, their primitive life and kindly manners endearing them to all true students of humanity, and the Nascopie Indians of the interior who visit the coast in summer and fall are the most primitive Indians of North America and will well repay those who are fortunate enough to meet and study them.

"We can give you a house for a base camp, furnished with necessary bedding, cooking outfit and food, also books and mechanical music for stormy days, a photo outfit, a small schooner, motor boat and canoes for travelling and hunting in the bays and rivers, tent, blankets, food, guns, ammunition, tobacco, guide, cook and porter. All you need to bring is fishing rods and tackle and any special gun, ammunition, tobacco or mosquito dope you may fancy. Travel light and have a good time getting there, free from worry about equipment. When you get there you have a wide choice of locations.

Innu (Indian) women along with Inuit and Settler ladies enjoy a warm day in late May at Richard White's trading post at Voisey's Bay. Photo by Richard White around 1930.

"How to get there – Take the train in any part of U.S.A. for St. John's, N.F. via North Sydney, C.B., one night from North Sydney on steamer to Port Aux Basques, N.F. thence train to St. John's, where you transfer to steamer for Nain, Labrador. There is also a direct steamer from New York to St. John's. On arrival of steamer at Nain we will meet you and take you 35 miles in motor boat to our base camp thro a most delightful inside passage resembling a section of the Inland Sea of Japan.

"Time to Come – Arrange to be in St. John's about the first week in July. Governed by ice conditions on Labrador, the mail steamer leaves for Nain about the 15th of July, some-times earlier or later. Time from St. John's to Nain about 10 days. In order to enjoy this unique trip properly you should be prepared to remain in the north till October.

"We limit the party to not fewer than 4 nor more than 6 men. Cost of trip per man $1000.00, (July to October) payable in advance at St. John's, N.F. This sum includes everything from the time you reach St. John's till you return to St. John's from north, but does not include expenses between your home and St. John's either way.

"If you are a genuine sportsman you'll take each day as it comes and travel the hardest road without getting mentally sore. If the mosquitoes are like bulldogs you'll lay it on the Gods of the Wilds and keep smiling. If you're going to be grouchy, get cold feet, or expect the fish to jump into the boat and the caribou and bears to grow on the trees, then take this trip at home in your easy chair, for hitting the trail in the big northern silences is no easy trip."

Since Dad wrote that back then, the tourism industry has flour-ished and Labrador is a great destination. The Crosbie family out of Newfoundland started camps in western Labrador in the late 1950's and, in the late 1960's, fishing and hunting camps built by the United States and Canadian military have sprung up south and north of

Goose Bay. Then chaps like Ray Cooper, Peter Paor, Bill Bennett, Bob Skinner and Jack Cooper established camps, and now today there are about fifty different destinations to choose from.

The author's wife Debby, with a healthy speckled brook trout, caught on a fly rod at Shapio Lake. This kind of fishing is accessible by floatplane in remote areas.

Many parts of Labrador, especially those with roads running through them are nearly fished out near the road area, there is still quite good fishing in remote places accessible by aircraft. If you think this is hard to believe, just ask someone who was in the Labrador City or Churchill Falls area in the 1960's and they'll tell you. Dick Budgell and Clancy Montague at Northwest River are a couple of fellows who have miles of experience and witnessed catching fish that had never seen a muddler or streamer fly in the life cycle of history. They can tell you what has happened to those stocks in the short span of 40 years! If you are interested in sport fishing in Labrador, we have several wonderful species that are a thrill and challenge to land.

In the western and inland areas, you can try your luck at catching Northern Pike, Lake Trout, Brook Trout, Splake (a cross between a Lake Trout and a Brook Trout), Whitefish, and Ounaniche (Waa-nan-nish meaning land-locked salmon). There are also the less popular species like common sucker and freshwater sculpin.

A word of caution about eating fish in areas where land has been flooded, like the Churchill Falls region. There is a consumption limit on fish in that area issued by health authorities because of elevated levels of mercury found in the fish there. From what I understand one would have to eat a lot on a continuous basis for quite a while before becoming sick. However, the cautionary word is out there.

There are bag limits and seasons, so check with your guide on those. In salt water, you can fish for sea run brook trout, Arctic char and Atlantic salmon. The Eagle River near Cartwright is probably the world's greatest salmon river, followed closely by the Adlotok and the Pinware. There are other rivers too like the Gilbert and Tom Luscombe. Minipi Camps operated by Jack and Lorraine Cooper offer some of the very best fishing for big brookies. This camp, like others, practices good conservation with its "catch and release" program and the stock remains healthy and plentiful with six to seven pound speckled trout commonly released.

The vast region north of Nain is a very good area for Arctic char and the fishing is excellent. It is accessible from Nain by chartering a local boat from Henry or Chesley Webb or from Tom Goodwin at the Atsanik Lodge. If you intend to fly in on float-equipped aircraft, it would be wise to become familiar with the weather patterns in that area. One of the most unpredictable elements in the region is the winds. They are very powerful in this mountain region and inexperienced flyers have had serious accidents and even loss of life. In the late 1990's, a Montreal group of fishermen were in Nachvak Lake, inside Nachvak Fiord. Powerful winds capsized their aircraft and they were killed. In August 2003, two other tourists crashed in the region and lost their lives. Two other hikers attempting to cross from Labrador to Quebec are missing as this book goes to print. It is wise to choose carefully when you are flying in that region and, if possible, take a local charter company with experience.

If you like to hunt, Labrador is home to big and small game. Caribou is the king of our land, while the moose has moved in over the past fifty years. Among the great hunting guides in Labrador are fellows like Don Mitsuk who works with Northern Lights Lodge out of Labrador City, Bruce Gear at Hopedale, the Webb brothers and John Merkuratsuk from Nain and others you will find in nearly every community. There's black bear hunting; polar bear hunting is limited to Inuit who have a quota of six animals a year for food and clothing purposes.

If you like smaller game, try spruce grouse, ruffed grouse or ptarmigan. If you like duck on a plate or Canada Goose, you can hunt for these in September. Rabbit and Arctic hare hunting is also good when the population cycle of these animals is up. Fishing in Labrador is best in inaccessible areas or where the user population is low. Where roads have been pushed through, the waters close to the roads have been all but fished out. For a good fishing trip, it is therefore best to take an aeroplane or helicopter and a guide, rough it out in a tent camp or go to a licensed outfitting camp. Jack Cooper's Minipi Camps, Powell's in Charlottetown or Vince Burton's on Flower's River are just a few of the thirty or so operators.

A Guiding Reflection

I guided one summer at the Park Lake camp south of Goose Bay. One particular week I was assigned to two chaps from the United States. One gent was a wealthy advertising company executive. One day we were below a set of rapids and he snagged "Labrador"…his spinner and hook got jammed between two rocks about a hundred and fifty feet from shore. After some unsuccessful tugging and some hearty cursing, I offered to take his rod and see if I could get it free. I walked downstream from the snagged hook and got it loose. As I rapidly reeled his hook in, I felt a strike, but nothing got on. Then I felt a strain on the rod. I continued reeling in and then I felt another strike. This one stayed on. I then handed the rod and reel to my fisherman and he kept reeling in. As his hook got closer he noticed it surface. To his amazement, there was no fish on his hook…there was another line! I had hooked his spinner into a line and hook that had been lost by another fisherman. That line had also worked free and while I started retrieving it for him, a fish got on the second line and hook. He landed the fish…a six and a half pound beautiful brookie! This man was pretty pleased to get his hook back, plus another hook and a prize brook trout as well. After his week was up, he and his party left on the Beaver floatplane. Back in the kitchen was an envelope for me and in it was a thank you note for a great fishing experience and a hundred dollar (U.S.) bill! This unusual experience is something that happens only once, so if you are considering fishing you can expect a good experience but don't expect them to jump into your boat!

Caribou on the ridge at Mistastin Lake, 120 km west of Davis Inlet.

ELEVEN

The Rhythm of the Land

Labrador is a treasure house of arts. For centuries Inuit and Innu have lived to the beat of caribou and sealskin drums. To hear and see Innu Elder Thomas Noah or the late Phillip Rich of Davis Inlet chant about the spirit of the caribou or Pien Penashue chant a rhythm of thanks to the Great Creator is an absolutely splendid thing.

My mother, Judy Hunter White, who was born at Nain Bay in 1902, was told by her family that the early Moravian missionaries working among the Inuit about a hundred years earlier chastised the Inuit for throat-singing and drum dancing. She was told in quiet whispers that the Labrador Inuit before her parents' time were ordered by the Missionaries to cease such activity, as it was "heathen" and "evil."

The practice has not been spoken of much in public and she said she was told the people were afraid of the missionaries. The early missionaries, Mom was told, used tactics like refusing to trade and cutting off Inuit from use of guns, traps and other necessities for hunting. They could also be refused other favours from the church. That's what my mother said of the disappearance of the drum from Labrador Inuit society.

Early Moravian Missionaries introduced brass band instruments to Labrador Inuit in the 1800's to play in church services and throughout the community during Christmas, Easter and other occasions. Photo courtesy of George Pauls.

One of my Innu friends, Rose Gregoire, tells me that the Roman Catholic priests tried the same with the Innu, but they, being more nomadic and living away from the settlements where the priest lived, managed to survive and keep their musical culture.

In the late 1990's, Gary Baikie and the Torngasok Cultural Society in Nain invited an Inuit man from Greenland to reintroduce drum dancing to Nain and Hopedale. Now the beat and rhythm of the Labrador Inuit has been brought alive and is well. Make it a must to take in a performance of the Nunatsiavut Drummers in Nain when you visit. Nain also is home to the Sundogs, a rock and roll band.

There is also music by singers Gerald Mitchell and Gary Mitchell of Makkovik. Makkovik has a very musical history and James Andersen and his relatives had local bands in the 1940's and '50's. Cartwright is home of singer Harry Martin. Other famous Cartwright

Mushua Innu Spirituality is best experienced through a Drum Song from Innu like Thomas Noah of Utshimatsits.

folk include poet and historian Leslie Pardy and boat builder Bruce Martin. Shirley Montague and her music come from her roots at Northwest River. The band, The Flummies, is a regular hit in the Lake Melville area. The Flummies came out of a group known as "the Best White Band in Town." This group was made up of Alton Best, his daughter Clarice, his son Maurice, his nephew Raymond and myself. We soon changed the name to the Flummies and other great musicians like Harris Learning, Bob Lunnen, the late George Shiwak and myself worked tirelessly and

The action and beat of the young Inuit drummers and dancers will fill your heart and soul.

helped put the band where it is today. In February 2003, the Flummies won the nomination of best Aboriginal group in the East Coast Music Awards, a recognition well deserved.

The group Black Spruce sprung up in the interior of Labrador and can be heard around Wabush and Labrador City. The Innu group, Michikamau from Sheshatshiu carries a special sound similar to Kashtin. Selby Mesher from Paradise River is a hit and he and his brother Ford just released a CD worth getting. Beatrice Hope's roots are at Kamarsuk and Nain and she adds a refreshing take of singing in Inuttut and English, as does the group Michikamau from Sheshatshiu. Beatrice too was a nominee at the ECMAs and came away without an award, but her time is coming. The songs of the late Byron Chaulk of Mulligan are found in the discs, records and tapes of every artist who has done a recording of Labrador music. "Old Mokami" is probably the best known of a number of songs Byron wrote before he died in the 1990's. If you can't find a concert on the go while you are visiting, then buy a recording of one of the artists mentioned and you won't be disappointed. The music goes with the land.

You will be safe in this region. By now you may have wondered where the name "the Big Land" came from. It came about in 1976, when I wrote a song about Labrador and our people and called it "The Big Land Song." I later used the term almost daily in reference to Labrador while I worked as a radio broadcaster at CBC Labrador in Happy Valley-Goose Bay. From there, it caught on, and many writers, broadcasters and others have and are using the term. Bill Flowers, a young lawyer originally from Rigolet, introduced a couple of hundred people to Labrador at a major fishery conference in 2001 at Happy Valley-Goose Bay by welcoming them to the Big Land, and took the moment to explain to them that I was the originator of the phrase so widely used today. Thanks Bill!

TWELVE

Activities in Summer

In summer, the sun sets quite late in Labrador, especially as you go farther north. In the most northerly region it remains light, as the sun will dip just below the horizon, so daylight remains. From the Nain area, south and westward, the sun will go well below the horizon but darkness in late June can last only three to four hours, which gives great, long days. Although the nights are short, they are not without the summer displays of the beautiful Northern Lights. It is said that Labrador offers one of the world's best chances to enjoy the Northern Lights as it has been calculated that they can be visible over 250 times a year. Some argue that the Northern Lights are better in winter than summer, but I must admit I have seen some spectacular displays in late July and August in the Nain area.

Canoeing

Summer is the time for long hiking adventures, fishing, camping, kayaking, canoeing or travelling by larger boats. Most canoeing is done in and around the towns of Wabush/Labrador City and Happy Valley-Goose Bay and in ponds and rivers along the southern Labrador and Trans-Labrador Roads.

You can leave the roadside at any time, and paddle the lakes to your heart's content. More experienced canoeists take a floatplane out of the larger centres and canoe down rivers to end up in one of the coastal communities. Menihek Lake is enormous and long and the great Ashuanipi (pronounce Ash-shwan-nip-ee), Lake Joseph and the Atikonak system through Ossokamanuan (Oh-sock-man-nu-one – say it quickly!) are great systems to enjoy in the western region of our "height of land."

Brian & Pat Green have enjoyed canoe trips in Labrador and in 2002 made the wise choice to abandon going through the Mouni Rapids on the Churchill River because of the danger. They will be back to enjoy more canoeing in Labrador next summer. In 2001 two men from Labrador City barely escaped with their lives when their canoe overturned while shooting rapids on the big river.

I know some guys from New York who went to the headwaters of the Kenamu and came out to Lake Melville. I've met others who left the headwaters of the Adlatok and went out to salt water and then turned north to Hopedale. Others have crossed from Kangiqsualujjuaq (meaning very large bay in Inuktitut) in Nunavik (northern Quebec) paddled up into the Labrador and out to Sudlek (Saglek) in northern Labrador. There are others who have taken the famous Churchill River down to Happy Valley-Goose Bay, camping and travelling on their own schedule and when the weather is good. Many experienced canoeists and paddlers will caution you about the sudden winds that can lash up the waters of our lakes and rivers. These "rogue" winds can appear with such speed and force that the surprise can put you in a frightening and dangerous situation.

Kayaking

Most advanced kayakers head for the coast and the Labrador Sea. Not many local Labrador people have kayaked in recent years, but there seems to be a rebirth in the sport. Richard Learning and his brother Jim kayaked from Happy Valley-Goose Bay out Lake Melville and south to their family home, Cartwright in Sandwich Bay in July 2002. Richard, also known as Dick, was delighted with his experience and even told me that he now prefers the kayak to the canoe. This is quite something as the Learnings, like many of the Labrador families, used the canoe all their lives. He told me that one of his uncles was the last person to use a kayak in the Sandwich Bay area during the 1930's.

Of course, Inuit, including my grandfather Phillipus Hunter from Nain Bay, used kayaks as his chief method of travel up to about 1925. After the Inuit and coastal people began to buy motor driven boats from Newfoundland fishermen, the kayak was put aside.

There are some models of original sealskin-covered kayaks at the culture centres in Hopedale and Nain. Ask the local historic and culture people to let you have a look. There is also a traditional kayak on display at the Interpretation Centre in Northwest River where Mina Hibbs is the curator; she has a pretty good handle on Labrador culture. The Labrador Heritage Society is active in Labrador City-Wabush where over the years people like the late Steve Michelin and Merle Roberts worked hard to preserve the history of the area. Also, Joyce and Ed Montague are among the volunteers who have kept the efforts alive, and have helped a lot to see the new Gateway facility running in that area. Ed is a good source of information if you want to know about the minerals and rocks of Labrador; he can also tell you a lot about the trapping history of the "height of land," as we call the area. He has been also active in arousing interest in the old trading post locations of Fort MacKenzie and others in the same area. The Labrador Heritage Society has a branch in Northwest River where the society has restored the Hudson's Bay Company store and turned it into a museum.

Exploring, Mountaineering and Hiking

This wonderful land is a great place for anyone who wants to experience the sheer enjoyment of exploring for fun. Over many years now, Labrador has been studied by a whole range of scientists including ornithologists, botanists, climatologists, geologists and archaeologists.

The Fitzhugh Expedition

The history of our Aboriginal people has attracted many archaeologists from Memorial University and other Canadian and American scientists. The most notable American group to carry out extensive work over the past thirty years is the Smithsonian Institution from Washington, DC. Dr. William (Bill) Fitzhugh, his students and colleagues have spent over 25 years uncovering evidence and writing new chapters in the history of our people.

In the summer of 1976, Dr. Fitzhugh had a crew working north of Nain. Among one of his parties was a young archaeologist, Ann Abraham. Ms. Abraham had been working in Labrador a couple of prior seasons and was becoming quite a seasoned northern scientist. This particular season they were working in Ramah Bay and one fine day the party headed in different directions looking for evidence of Inuit activity.

After several hours, Ms. Abraham did not return at the agreed upon time. A search by her co-workers and by a geological survey party found no trace. Two days after she was reported missing, Dr. Stephen Loring and Ann's brother flew to Ramah Bay along with a Canadian Search and Rescue helicopter based out of Halifax. Search and Rescue made an extensive air search of the rugged topography to no avail. Nor did Loring and his companions find any trace after a ground search that lasted several days. Eventually, an RCMP helicopter was sent to Ramah to return with the search party. The RCMP arrived with a Zodiac for a detailed water search along the imposing cliff face, but again, no trace of Ms. Abraham was ever found.

Every possible hill, valley and shore was carefully searched and it was thought she might have slipped and fallen over a cliff into the fiord. A polar bear was spotted in the area at the same time she disappeared and it was thought she might have been attacked and devoured by the bear. The Mounties wanted to kill the bear to see if there was any evidence of human remains, but the bear was not seen again and it was not pursued. To this day, the fate of Ms. Ann Abraham remains an unsolved mystery. Again, this story only reinforces the importance to travel in pairs or as a group and not alone.

If you are interested in mountain climbing, there is a chap in Nain who I recommend you contact. Paul Fenton is an experienced mountain guide, and has much local knowledge to add to his own experience. Paul can guide you in this type of activity and northern Labrador has some of the most untouched mountain climbing potential in Canada. Our mountains peak between three and almost six thousand feet, or two thousand metres. These areas are accessible by charter boat out of Nain or, if you have the money like Bill Gates, then chartering aircraft from Goose Bay would be the ticket. Interestingly, Bill Gates did charter a couple of helicopters from Goose Bay and went to the Torngat Mountains for a few days camping and hiking in 1998.

There are some other wondrous places that might be a bit easier on the pocketbook than an excursion to the Torngat Mountains. Between Rigolet and Cartwright lies a seventy-five-kilometre stretch of sandy coast. Some call it the Porcupine Strand and others call it the Wonderstrand or just plain "the Strand." This is accessible by hiring a local boat in summer from Rigolet or Cartwright. Check with a reliable boat owner to check out the cost and time involved, or with

George Barrett at Cartwright who runs a great kayaking and adventure tour service there.

The Iron Strand, south of Ryan's Bay, northern Labrador. The sandy beach consists of the hard mineral garnet, used as an abrasive. Photo courtesy of Leroy Metcalfe.

Then there's the Muskrat Falls on the Churchill River. About twenty miles or so west of Happy Valley-Goose Bay, it lies about two kilometres south of the main Trans-Labrador road. While not as impressive and thunderous as the 245-foot drop at the original Hamilton Falls I visited in 1962, this seventy-five foot drop in the river is still a powerful combination of rapids and waterfalls. If you want to get a view of Lake Melville, you can also hire a boat or snowmobile from Jock Campbell at Northwest River and go visit Mokami Hill. From this 900-foot bald mountain you can see for miles and miles. Along the coast there's the old whaling station remains of the Norwegian Whaling Company at Hawke's Harbour. Then there's the Hole-In-The-Wall, a tunnel carved by the ocean through a solid cliff. Again, this amazing feature is accessible by a sixteen-mile boat ride from Charlottetown.

Robert and Sharon Langdon of Happy Valley-Goose Bay enjoy the bike and walking trails which run from one end of the town to the other.

Walking

If you are not into these more aggressive sports, there is plenty of good easy walking in and around all the communities and towns. In Happy Valley-Goose Bay you won't see any sidewalks (except on Grenfell Street); instead there is a network of walking and biking routes, located about fifteen to twenty metres from the streets; these are paved.

This most useful network is great for casual or serious walking, running or jogging and is the brainchild of former mayor Henry (Hank) Shouse. It's also great for a bike ride and runs about twenty kilometres from one end of the town to the other.

Festivals and Events

The Bakeapple Festival in southern Labrador is one of the longest running in the province. This five-day event includes music, local arts and crafts, sightseeing and of course, a taste of the local berry, the bakeapple. The bakeapple is also called loganberry. Along the

Straits there is much to take in like the famous lighthouse at Point Amour, off which lies the wreck of the British Navy warship, *Raleigh*, which ran aground and broke up on a shoal in Forteau Bay. Eleven men died in the event, which was the result of urgent navy business that had to be carried out: the top officers of the ship were going salmon fishing on the Forteau River!

Of course, there is Red Bay where you can go back even farther in time and see the signatures of the Basque Whalers. The Beach Festival at Northwest River is another event, highlighting music, culture and foods. There are others like canoe races at Goose Bay and the regatta at Labrador City and Wabush. The smaller communities have more modest events but are no less as exciting or vibrant. The settlement of West St. Modeste, where Agnes Pike is from, is one of the oldest along that coastline. Agnes has spent much of her life volunteering as a community leader in her town. Then there's Stelman Flynn who also devoted much time to local politics, and in Mary's Harbour you'll find Ford Rumbolt, another tireless fighter for community improvements in the area.

The little Village of Mud Lake on the Hamilton River downstream from Happy Valley-Goose Bay is accessible only by boat in summer or snow machine over river ice in winter. Mud Lake holds a fair every June to support and maintain its little church. The village is also the historic site of Labrador's first commercial timber operation; Dickie Lumber Company of Nova Scotia set up a steam powered sawmill and lumber operation there around 1900.

Long-time resident Susan Felsberg (she from England and her husband Hans from Europe) has amassed a most interesting account of the operation and its demise.

The Trout Festival in Makkovik is a good example of a festival in a small town setting and there are many others. By late August, the feel of fall is evident in the air and soon the brilliant crimson and yellows of the north will be in full display. By taking in events like these and meeting local people, you'll learn a lot more about the rich past and vibrant present of Labrador.

NATO military jets parked at Goose Bay Airport.

If you should be out camping, you may hear some rumbling in the distance, which sounds different from thunder. It's the military jets out of Goose Bay that, from April to October, are in low and high-level flight training. When they are low you don't hear them coming until they are immediately overhead or just past. They can make a deafening roar and, if you are not expecting them, they can give you an awful scare. They use Goose Bay because the population in Labrador is small and scattered. Although they can fly over areas where few people live, we are still out there. We always use and need the land.

I guess you could say I am a casual, novice prospector always looking at rocks. One summer my wife and I were prospecting and camped at Harp Lake. We told the military coordinators in Goose Bay that we would be there and they promised that their planes would not fly over us. But they are known to sometimes forget where they are. These noisy machines flying fifty feet over your head can make you reach for the ass of your pants to see if it happened!

Back in Goose Bay the local people take the constant take-offs and landings of these winged engines in their stride. Visitors seem to like the novelty of having their own air show. One visitor I met from Ontario, Max Henning, was quite delighted to see the formations and speed, but remarked, "Can't they find a muffler for these things?"

The Goose Bay airport has a history going back to 1938/39. It was built for aircraft to land on when going to or coming from Europe and the Second World War theatre. It has seen almost every imaginable aircraft in the world. In May 1980, the space craft *Enterprise* and its transporter aircraft, a Boeing 747, landed at Goose Bay on its way to the air show in Paris, France. It was the first and only time a US spacecraft was ever on Canadian soil!

Golfers in the photo enjoy the summer sun at the Amaruk Golf Course in Happy Valley/Goose Bay.

If you are a golfer, you have two opportunities to play in Labrador. There is a nine-hole course called Amaruk (meaning wolf in Inuttut) Golf Club in Happy Valley-Goose Bay, and the eighteen-hole Tamarack (named after a type of tree like a larch tree which is called a "juniper" tree in Newfoundland and Labrador) Golf Course in Labrador City.

The beginnings of the golf course in Goose Bay are most interesting in that one of the original people who worked hard to start the Amaruk was a fellow by the name of Ernie Funsten. Ernie came to Goose Bay with the Federal Department of Transportation (DOT in those days). The unusual twist about this development was that Ernie had only one arm, yet he persisted and saw his dream of a golf course in Labrador come true. He was also able to play a very competitive round despite his physical handicap.

THIRTEEN

Activities in Winter

This Big Land is a vast region and although the sun rises for fewer hours in winter, its rays make the snow-covered land sparkle with millions of diamonds in the snow. The long, cold nights also regularly offer the Northern Lights in the star-filled sky. The green, pink, and purple lights weave and spin, sometimes with a gentle flow and sometimes a quickened dance across the heavens.

When we were growing up near Nain, these mystical lights were used by our parents to stop us from playing outside too late. We were told that the Northern Lights could come down and sweep children into the sky and take them away. It is also said that the dancing lights are sky people playing in the dark. Whistling out loud at them can make them dance and move even more. You don't believe it? Come and give your whistle a try sometime.

Snowmobiling and Dogsledding

Snowmobiling is a growing activity in Labrador and there is now a network of groomed trails from western Labrador, eastward toward Goose Bay; from Goose Bay the trail runs both north and south. The southern trail takes in all communities south of the Mealy Mountains and the northern route goes to Rigolet, Makkovik and Postville. Many coastal people like to follow the old dog team trails and routes used by mailmen and local people. There is also dogsledding, down-hill and cross-country skiing, fishing through the ice, caribou and small game hunting, and hunting for the camouflaged ptarmigan.

Mother Nature provides this bird with the ability to turn like the snows in the winter and brown like the land in the summer. This ptarmigan is a male as the red marks over the eyebrow indicate.

Today there is a good choice of dogsled races to enjoy. Labrador City and Wabush hold the Labrador 120 in early March. St. Lewis holds the Ronald Strugnell Memorial Dogteam Race, and Port Hope Simpson holds a dogteam race during its Snow Bash Winter Festival. One of the smallest communities, William's Harbour, is the starting and ending point of a hundred mile race held each year. This event takes about two days' travelling through several communities along the way. There's the Easter Monday Dogteam Race at Makkovik, which originated in 1935, and at nearby Postville there's the Easter Festival Dogteam Race. In Hopedale, the Ethel Pijogge Memorial Race is held around late March or early April, and Rigolet celebrates one of its World War I veterans through the Levi Pottle Memorial Race. At the Labrador Winter Games there's the H.J. Williams Memorial Dogteam Race held every third year. The next race in that weeklong event will be in March of 2006.

Many of these races have grown from the first dog sled revival held in the early 1970's when Richard Learning, Carl Saunders and myself organized the original Labrador Heritage Cup dogsled race in Happy Valley-Goose Bay. At that time, the snowmobile had replaced all but less than a dozen of the wonderful and mighty Labrador sled dogs. The Labrador Heritage Cup was donated by Melvin Woodward to the Labrador Heritage Society. Max Blake, Uncle Jim Learning, and William Wolfrey drove the three teams to race in that first Labrador Heritage Cup event in 1979. Max gathered up a few dogs including the sole remaining dog that Carl Saunders had left from his family's team. Uncle Jim Learning still kept a couple and with the help of Richard (Dick) and Carl he gathered up a few more from William Wolfrey and we were on our way. Max took first place, William Wolfrey second, and Uncle Jim Learning took third place.

The event was designed to make people aware that the Labrador sled dog was nearing extinction and the race demonstrated the importance of keeping our dogs from almost vanishing from our history. In the three years following, people like Douglas Jacque, Michael Best, Hubert Groves and Henry John Williams took up the interest and, since then, other people have raised dogs and the population is back to a healthy and stable number.

After the second year, I arranged for the engraving area of the cup to be enlarged so that there would be plenty of space to engrave names for many years to come. When my time as volunteer at the Labrador Heritage Society came to an end, people like Elsie Johnson and John McGrath took up the slack on the traces and carried on the events. I was Vice President of the Society at the time and after the first year, we decided that it would be fitting to let each winner of the cup take it back to his or her home community for a month or two and then send it back to the Labrador Heritage Society in Goose Bay for safekeeping, until the following winner could take it home for a short time.

Names like Max Blake of Rigolet, Douglas Jacque of Postville, Hubert Groves of Makkovik, Kenny Pottle of Rigolet and Henry John Williams of Cartwright are engraved on the cup. In Rigolet alone, there are seven teams. Other names you'll see on the cup include Douglas Jacque of Postville who spent his whole life, like Henry John, depending on sled dogs. Of the younger drivers, Kenny Pottle of Rigolet has won the Heritage cup the most times and Kenny and his teams hold some of the fastest times. Up to that time, the Labrador husky dog was facing extinction because the teams had been abandoned in preference to the snowmobile. Less than sixty years ago, the Labrador husky dog was the vital part of life on our coast. The dog population then was around 30,000 dogs and 5,000 people.

Labrador Winter Games, 2003.

My father, Richard White, who lived in our house and trading post at Voisey's Bay from 1913 to 1958, wrote in 1940, "despite modern inventions, the dog team is still the most reliable form of transport over the frozen bays and snow covered barrens. Every driver boasts of the prowess of his team be it five dogs or a dozen and many are the arguments over the merits of the respective teams. In proportion to its size, the dog's hauling power is wonderful. Its endurance is even more so and teams have often covered 80 miles in one continuous run of seventeen hours on a spring day. After a feed of seal and a night's rest they made the return journey in the same time. The Labrador hunter must prepare and maintain his property and equipment in the fall for the coming harsh winter. Perhaps the most important is the care of his dog team and equipment for without his dogs the Labrador native is almost helpless."

Today's dog owners have teams for the love of keeping these great dogs and you will see a reflection in today's owners of the pride and care that my father experienced and wrote about.

Dogsled races. Labrador Winter Games.

Some of our dogs out to haul back a load of firewood in this 1945 photo taken by my father Richard White.

While we have managed to save our dog teams, the snowmobile has become the winter way of transportation. Groomed snowmobile trails lead through all the little communities and settlements along the southern Labrador coast. If you get to Charlottetown, see if you can meet Mr. Ben Powell. He founded the community and has written over fifteen books since his first one, *Labrador By Choice*. While you are in Charlottetown you might also ask to chat with Earl Stone. They and others like the Wentzells, Powells and Campbells know a lot about history of the region.

Snowshoeing

If you are hiking or on snowshoes, avoid going too close to waterfalls or fast running water. The steam and spray that rises above a waterfall drops back around the area and becomes pure hard ice. In 1970, two men and their wives decided to snowshoe out to the Churchill Falls. At that time the falls were still in their natural state and the steam vapour cloud could be seen twenty miles away. The men got too close to the icy surface and they slid helplessly down into the open gorge 200 feet below while their wives watched in shock and horror. The two men's bodies were never found. These are the dangers lurking around rivers and water falls in winter.

Winter Carnivals

There are other attractions, like the winter carnivals. The Goose Bay winter carnival is the longest running such event in Canada and North America. It was started by the Royal Canadian Air Force in 1943 to help break the long winter with some entertainment and activity. Winter is when the schools' students present the plays they have collectively written about their lives and communities at the Labrador Creative Arts Festival, which has also been running for twenty-seven years. Running since 1983, the Labrador Winter Games takes place every three years in Happy Valley-Goose Bay. The weeklong events brings athletes from every community across the land and besides the excitement of the daily contests, the open-

Site of Labrador Winter Games.

All ages enjoy a smooth snowmobile ride on the groomed trails.

ing ceremonies are always sold out within a couple of hours after tickets go on sale. While the games are about trying to win, the spirit of the event brings people together and it is also a time to showcase our art and culture. For a well-rounded, healthy, fresh air vacation, this is one of the best in the province.

There are new winter festivals emerging as well. There are events in western Labrador, the Happy Valley-Goose Bay area and in southern communities. These are centred on the snowmobile and the groomed snowmobile trails sprouting up across the region.

Winter is the longest season in this Big Land and while it can be bitterly cold, the days tend to be sunny, and being there can be a pleasurable and healthy experience. Be sure to dress properly for cold winter action and you will enjoy Labrador's impressive setting and peaceful silence. After all, what's better than a steaming bowl of winter-killed caribou stew and a mug of hot chocolate around the comfort of a wood burning stove after a day out in the cleanest, freshest air, far to the north of big cities.

Silent Dangers – Avalanches

This chapter is not intended to give you the chills and raise your fears to the point that you won't venture outside your hotel or accommodation; it is intended to help you respect this beautiful land and be aware of some dangers you would neglect at your peril.

The main dangers of travelling in Labrador during winter are getting caught in blizzards, avalanches, landslides, rock slides, getting lost, falling through ice (we call it going through ice), and freezing. Snow blindness and carbon monoxide poisoning are secondary dangers. The main rule is never travel alone and always tell someone where you are going and when you expect to be back. As much as possible, stick to your intended route and, if you get that lost feeling, stop right where you are and make yourself comfortable.

Almost all communities have volunteer search and rescue teams that work closely with the RCMP and the Provincial Emergency Measures organization. The volunteers who constitute those teams

are extremely experienced travellers and have often put themselves at risk in searching for lost and overdue people. Poor planning and haste instigate most searches. Norman Andersen is the leader of the volunteer Search and Rescue group in Nain. He says visitors should check with him and his group or with the RCMP before going into the wilderness to let them know where they intend to go. Plan you trip carefully and check with reliable local people about the area where you are going and how to best get there. He says always let someone know where you are going and when you expect to be back.

It is important to realize that even though it is 40 below, there are still places where there is open water and unsafe ice. This is why it is so important to have a reliable and experienced guide to travel with over the ice and snow. All along the coast there are what we call "tickles" between islands or between islands and mainland where the

Ice on the salt water in the spring near Nain.

water rushes through like a river as the tides rise and fall. The water moves with such force that these places never freeze over. We call them "rattles" because of the noise and racket that can be heard coming from them during rising and falling tide peaks. If you are on a snowmobile and don't know where these danger areas are and where the ice is thin, your ignorance could be fatal. Around Nain and Voisey's Bay, for example, up to twenty of these weak spots have been identified in a five-mile radius alone. With changes in climate our hunters and travellers are these days observing dangerous areas where it is normally safe.

During the exploration part of the Voisey's Bay mineral discovery just south of Nain; the winter of 1995/96 was not an unusual winter. The weather was clear and cold with average snowfall. The companies overseeing the exploration camp, Archaean Resources and Diamond Fields Resources, had to use the airstrip in Nain for all their air services, as there was no runway for aircraft on the land near the site. When winter freeze-up came it was decided to build a runway on the sea ice near the Anaktalak Bay camp at Edward's Cove.

The natural ice thickness is usually about five feet, but it was decided that they would top that up by flooding the ice, thus gaining further thickness and allowing for larger aircraft on skis to operate from the ice. Every so often, when needed, a heavy snowplow grader would be sent out to remove the snowdrifts and smooth the airstrip. One day in March, the routine activities took place, but suddenly the heavy bulldozer broke through the ice. The operator never had a chance of escaping and went down with the machine and drowned. It appears that the unwary dozer operator strayed beyond the parameters of the built-up ice field and went through.

Inuit know that seawater or saltwater ice thickness is not constant in areas where there are strong tides and moving water. Saltwater ice can be four feet thick in one place, but perhaps twenty metres away it might only be three feet thick. It is important to measure ice every five to ten metres to check for any great differences. Freshwater ice is more constant in thickness but it's not as flexible as ice containing salts. I remember when Wheeler Airlines and Eastern Provincial Airways (EPA) used to call along the coast to ask people to take ice measurements for them. For the Beaver on skis they needed eight inches in the fall and winter and for the Otter they needed twelve inches. As winter pressed on into March, pilots and contacts in the villages increased their observations as time moved toward spring. By late-April and early-May, ski operations were under close and careful scrutiny.

When most people think of avalanches their minds turn to the Rocky Mountains on the west coast of Canada. Labrador in winter has hundreds of avalanches and snow slides. In summer, there are numerous rock or landslides. When you are travelling around the Anaktalak or Voisey's Bay areas you will see ample potential avalanche sites, especially as you pass along hillsides and around steep islands and narrow mountain valleys.

There are many old stories and legends of people being killed by snow. These are handed down to us. In my old hometown of Nain, we always kept a keen eye out for avalanches. The slopes of Nain Hill behind the houses are a natural site for avalanches, and we had them every year.

Our people have been recording and noting them for years and years and, recently, two chaps, David Liverman and Martin Batterson have been collecting records of incidents. They work at the provincial department of Mines and Energy at St. John's. They have a list of forty-two cases recorded since 1782, and a total number of sixty-one fatalities. One of the worst incidents occurred on the Nain hill slope in 1782 causing twenty-two deaths.

Avalanches have hit people from villages in southern Labrador to the northern tip of the region. Aside from the incidents back in the 1700's and 1800's, one of the more recent tragedies was at Ullik, a small homestead near Nutak, north of Nain, in 1936. Sam and Bella

Lyall told the story to their daughters Jessie Ford and Christine Baikie of Nain. The sisters relayed the story to me.

On a March morning, Joe Milley and his wife Paulina were carrying out their morning chores. "Paulina was a crippled woman," recalls Christine, "and I always remember her because she amazed us on how she was able to get around. There were no crutches like today…all she had was like a piece of board she would place in front of herself to get from one place to another."

In the house, the extended family included Sara Townley, Simeon Kohlmeister and his wife, Eva, and their son John Kohlmeister. Also present were Cornelius Ulvoriak and his wife, Carolyn, and their relative Hulda Zarpa with her infant, Abba. As the story goes, suddenly and without warning, around 11:00 A.M., a huge ball of snow came down the treeless hill behind the house. The giant ball shot right through the dwelling. Everything in its path went with it.

"Uncle Ernie went to Nutak that day for supplies and came back to Tessiuak to get help," recalls Jessie. Ernie Lyall got his brother Sam to join him and on two dog teams they headed for Ullik. "When they got there, two people had died and one was missing," Jessie added. "Simon Kohlmeister and Carolyn Ulvoriak were killed by the crash. Carolyn was knitting at the time and her body was recovered with several knitting needles found driven into her arms and body. Sara Townley was buried, yet alive; they could not find her at first and had her given up for dead."

It is a miracle that anyone lived. Christine recalls her father Sam describing the scene. "Abba Zarpa was just an infant and his mother Hulda was breast-feeding him at the moment the avalanche crashed upon them. They were sitting by the wood-cooking stove. The baby got scalded from a pot of hot water and burned badly by the fire but he lived. Eva and John Kohlmeister survived, and Joe Milley adopted young John and raised him."

There were other miracles in the tragic event. "Sara Townley was on the floor mixing bread in a pan at the time the avalanche struck," Jessie added, "and she found herself standing upright buried under the snow." Sara later told the rescuers that she could hear them and she kept alive by blowing upwards with her breath and the snow kept melting until she broke through. "She was under the snow for almost two days," Christine recalled.

And what about Joe's wife, Paulina, the crippled lady? "She was sitting in the wicker-type chair she always sat in," said Jessie, "and she was found out on the harbour ice, still in the chair, not a scratch on her or the chair!" The house was destroyed and the survivors moved in with other families until spring. By fall Joe Milley had another house built.

There was another avalanche in the late 1970's at Hopedale. A large number of schoolchildren were playing and sliding on the hillside by the village. The overhanging snow ridge let go and two youngsters were buried. The fast action of a schoolteacher; walking home from classes and hearing the roar, he grabbed a snow shovel and saved the two youngsters from suffocation by digging them out.

In summer, rock and landslides are another danger to watch for. In January 2003, a group of RCMP officers and their wives narrowly escaped serious injury at Natsâluk, a narrow pass on the overland trail leading from Nain toward Kauk Harbour, and on to the Voisey's Bay mining site at Anaktalak Bay. Natsâluk means "steep cliff or embankment" and this cliff towers about 900 metres above you as you pass through the narrow lead. It is also called "the blow hole" and has always been known to Nain people as a very dangerous place for avalanches. Every year there are snow slides which, depending on the severity and size of the event, completely or partially cover the narrow trail. As a youngster, I remember travelling through there on dog team and at times when the snow conditions were considered unstable, we would avoid going this route and travel to and from Nain on the sea ice. Natsâluk is a place I always give a visual check and constant observation for likely avalanche.

FOURTEEN

Perils in Cold Weather

Hypothermia is caused by exposure to cold and is aggravated by dampness, wind and exhaustion. Signs to look for are uncontrollable shivering, slurred speech and stumbling. Unnoticed, it can lead to collapse and death. Medical people say the best treatment is to return the body temperature to its normal range. They recommend a hot bath and drying with a rough towel. Out on the land where there are no luxuries like a hot bathtub, the person should be taken to shelter and bedded down. If no kind of heating unit is available, strip the person of clothing and place a naked person on each side of the victim, keeping them well covered by blankets, skins, and any cover to retain heat. There are stories of frozen people who were apparently dead being restored to life after many hours of this kind of care.

If you plan a winter trip, look around the communities for reliable and experienced people. The community knows who these people are. Check with the local fisheries or wildlife guardians, the community council office or the RCMP. Reliable hunters and travellers know where best to camp safely. Even in an emergency they will not camp on certain sea ice. Even at -70°, sea ice can break away and drift off into the north Atlantic.

In the early 1980's, a pilot was ferrying a small aircraft from Europe to the United States. Goose Bay was his first stop after crossing the ocean. As he neared Labrador he hit headwinds and ran out of fuel, but he landed safely on wheels on the sea ice east of Rigolet. He was picked up before nightfall by a rescue helicopter. The next day he arranged for a helicopter to fly him and some fuel to the spot where he had abandoned the aircraft. They reached the location, but all there was to be seen was the broad blue expanse of the Labrador Sea.

If you are looking for original winter living like our Inuit fore-parents did, check out fellows like Paul Nochasak, Jacko Merkeratsuk or his son Eli, who are accomplished at building snow houses, or igloos, for a camp. A night in an igloo is a once-in-a-lifetime experience. Once you crawl inside, it opens up like an upside-down bowl. The room is soundproof, much like a radio broadcasting studio and you can see your breath but you will not freeze, as your body heat will warm up the inside. You can sleep on caribou, black bear or polar bear skins for a most comfortable night. It will be an experience you can tell others about for the rest of your life!

The Labrador coast in winter showing the flow edge or sina, the Inuktitut word for edge of the ice. The position of ice edge is constantly changing from the forces of ocean storms and temperature changes.

There are many people in Labrador who can tell you about snow-blindness. Snow-blindness, which is severe irritation and extreme pain when one looks toward light, is caused by the sun's rays that are either direct, or reflected from snow, ice or water. Light of unusually high intensity, with the higher-than-normal percentages of ultra-violet characteristic of northern sunlight, strikes the eye from below where it is not protected by eyelids or lashes. Without protection, you can become snow-blind within a couple of hours. The only protection is to wear snow goggles that stop this light from getting through. Older methods include goggles carved from wood with small slits that worked quite effectively.

The cure is to protect light-damaged eyes from further light and to relieve the pain. Stay in a dark room. My mother put cold cloths on my eyes, but many older folks used damp tealeaves from the teapot. When the Tetley tea bag was changed from being square to the round shape they are today, Uncle Henry Dicker of Nain held one up and said to me, "Look Winston, they thought about Labrador people when they made these. They are just the right fit over the eye!" You should recover in twelve to eighteen hours.

Carbon monoxide poisoning is another danger, because of the use of small engines and cars in the winter. This gas is very dangerous and can kill. The signs are dizziness, headache, nausea, and drowsiness. If you should break down on the road and then use your car or truck engine for warmth, you should first check to make sure your exhaust pipes are clear of snow, and also roll down your windows as it could be fatal to stay in a vehicle with the engine running and the windows closed. Avoid parking close to buildings where snow can build up to block your exhaust.

In the early 1970's at the Churchill Falls construction camp, there was a fatal and tragic ending for several people living in a staff-housing trailer. One evening a resident parked his car with the tail pipe to the dwelling; he did not notice that he had backed so far into the bank that the rear bumper of the car and the tail pipe were buried in the snow bank surrounding the trailer. These trailers were on wood foundations. The heat from the tail pipe melted a tunnel through the snow and the engine exhaust spread under the building and then rose up into the trailer. The next day all the inhabitants were found dead slumped in chairs or in their beds. They had all fallen asleep from the carbon monoxide poison, which came from the idling automobile.

Sadly, it seems that it takes tragic events like this to remind us of the silent dangers around us; we can only hope that these stories can help prevent these accidents and save lives.

Storms can rise and appear quickly in this land. In northern Labrador great forces of Mother Nature can lash out; winds can whip up into a raging blizzard within hours. To get caught in the middle of one of those can be deadly and tragic. Harvey Saunders, who was born at Daniel's Rattle and a surviving brother of one of the young men in this story, and the late George Dicker of Nain refreshed my memory of a story that occurred when I was five years old living in Voisey's Bay and Kauk Harbour.

The Saunders and Ford Story

On February 3, 1946 Allan Saunders, age 19, left from the Saunders homestead at Daniel's Rattle south of Voisey's Bay. His intention was to get a komatik sled load of seals at Nain, pick up some provisions, visit relatives and return to Daniel's Rattle with his load. Along the way Chesley John Ford, age 13, from the Ford's homestead joined Allan because he wanted to go along for the trip. For this trip Allan had to use one of his older dogs as leader because his regular leader was left at home as it was crippled after it had been caught by the leg in a fox trap. The pair arrived at the Winter's homestead at Kamarsuk near Voisey's Bay. The day was mild but in the air there was a sign of oncoming weather. The Winters suggested that the two stay in case the weather got bad before they reached Nain. As they were only about five hours run on dogs from Nain, the two decided to have tea and move on. By early afternoon the winds drove the snow into a ferocious blizzard, the temperature dropped, and it was bitterly cold. The storm lasted two full days and nights before calm returned.

After the fury ended, John's brother, Thomas Ford, came from Boat Harbour via Kamarsuk to Nain to see if his brother and Allan had made it through the storm. Tom got a shock when he got to Nain and learned that they had not arrived. Search parties were sent out. They came to our homestead at Kauk Harbour, about eight miles from where the Voisey's Bay Project camp is today at Anaktalak Bay.

George Dicker was among the searchers and he had Rev. William Peacock, Dan Henoche and a Newfoundland Ranger with him.

After checking our place, George decided to work south along the route the two travellers would have taken. The day before the search, although it was still pretty stormy, George had walked on snowshoes seven miles to a small island next to Kauk Island and Kauk Bluff where he had some fox traps. There was still high, drifting snow that day, and he could only see the tops of hills, but he recalled something that had caught his keen eye. He told me, "I remember thinking I had seen some obscure dog footin' on the ice near my fox trap and I took it to be the track of someone's dog from Nain." There were hundreds of dogs in Nain at that time, as everyone had anywhere from ten to twenty dogs and often a few dogs would run away for a couple of days before returning home.

George and the searchers reached the small island just south of our homestead where Dad (Richard White) had one of his trading posts. George stopped his team on the southern end of the small island to walk the half-mile to his fox trap at the other end. As he neared the area of his fox trap, he thought he heard the howl of a dog and dismissed it as being one of his own dogs behind him. A few minutes later, he crossed over what he thought were some old komatik tracks. "The first thing I noticed was that the komatik tracks were wide...wide like a komatik used by people from south of here. Us Nain people had narrow komatiks," George noted.

When he got to his fox trap, he was surprised to find a dog caught in it. He didn't want to shoot the trapped dog so he found a small stick. With it he gave the dog a blow over the head and the dog fell into a seemingly lifeless lump on the hard driven snow. "The Ranger asked me if I had killed 'en and I said he is just knocked out. He'll come around after." George released the dog's paw from the trap. When the dog regained consciousness, it took off toward the shore near a big rock. When it reached the area of the rock a whole team of dogs suddenly emerged from under the snow and the bally caters

The late George Dicker found the remains of the two young victims of the killer blizzard.

(ice chunks). They knew then that they had found the team belonging to the overdue travellers.

George and the Ranger reached the huge boulder and on the opposite side they discovered the young man and boy. "The older boy, Allan, was lying on the snow with his arms across his chest and his hands covering his face. He looked like he was alive, but he was dead. A few feet away we found a pile of blankets and clothing. The youngster was partly covered by this. He too was dead. Both had stopped by the big boulder and perished," George explained as though it had happened just yesterday.

No one knows for sure what really happened, but Harvey Saunders believes that Allan didn't have complete confidence in the dog team leader as it was an older dog and was unfamiliar with the Nain area. The Saunders family figured that Allan stopped the team to wait out the storm as he feared that the leader might lead them astray. Harvey says that if the original leader crippled from the fox trap was in the team, Allan would have had the confidence in it and the dog would have led the team straight to our house at Kauk Harbour because that leader had been at our place many times.

George also figured that if they were familiar with the Nain area, the dogs would have taken them to our house at Kauk or even on to Nain. The two victims were just two miles from our house, and five miles from Nain. Word was sent by dog team to the families and the two young people were laid to rest in Nain.

Another Vicious Storm

In January 1979, a group of nine caribou hunters from Nain were caught in another sudden storm high on the treeless tundra west of Okak Bay. The weather turned bad not long after they left on the ninth. On the fourteenth, it cleared up for a short while but they didn't get any caribou. On the fifteenth, the weather started to worsen into drifting snow and the party turned back to reach the shelter and protection of trees down in a valley. Within an hour there was a howling blizzard. The conditions grew even worse as the north wind-gusts made standing up impossible. The visibility was reduced so badly that they could not even see below their knees, nor farther than a hand in front of their faces. The hunters' hands and feet began to freeze.

The storm turned so vicious that their snowmobiles choked up and the engines failed to run. One by one, they gave out. They tried to cover themselves with a tent from one of the komatiks, but in minutes they were covered in snow and had to get out. By now all their hunting gear and equipment was also buried or lost in the snow. The men were soon forced to walk, which was treacherous. They would be trudging along not knowing if the next step would be over the edge of a five-foot embankment or a five hundred-foot fall over a cliff. By nightfall they came to a bunch of trees. To fall asleep was to invite disaster, so with just the trees for cover they held up there for the night.

The next morning they started off again. In the afternoon of that day, the wind was so vicious that they could not stand up. At one point they were on the clear, windswept ice of a brook or river, and the wind blew them onto their hands and knees. Under these conditions, they all became separated and three hunters somehow found themselves away from the other six.

Nightfall came and the group of three hunters finally made it to a tent they had left on the way into the hunting grounds. There was a stove in the tent and they took care of themselves as best they could. Worried and uneasy about the well being of the rest of their hunting companions, they were making plans to search for them when they heard someone hollering. Three more of the party had arrived and they broke the terrible news that the other three companions had perished.

On the seventeenth, the six hunters still alive were in the tent. On the morning of the eighteenth, the weather began to clear and three men left to walk to the coast for help. Weak, hungry, and half-frozen, they walked and crawled for eighteen hours without stopping. They made it to Nutak where they knew people to be staying. They mixed up what gasoline they could to get back to their three companions in the tent. The storm was of such force that people in Nain were worried and they asked the RCMP to go to Nutak. The police arrived just in time and took the other three survivors back to Nain. Search teams later recovered two of the bodies, but the youngest man was never found. This was another sad occasion in the long history of tragic times that can come upon us in Labrador.

Such are the dangers of this land that it is wise for newcomers not to travel without good advice, and even then to travel in the company of skilled and reputable local people. Now that more and more visitors and mining workers are coming to Labrador, we hope they will respect the skills and knowledge of our local people. When you arrive in our communities, take the time to visit the local council offices and let people know whom you are and where you are going. When you show respect in this way, our people will admire and respect you as well and look after you.

FIFTEEN

Travel Overland and by Sea

When you are using the land you must take good care to protect yourself and the land. Plan carefully and with the assistance of reliable local people. Ask people for their opinion and get them to show you the best things to do and where to go. Local traditional knowledge should be respected as natural hazards can test your personal physical condition, equipment and wilderness experience to their limits.

A Cross-country Adventure

A good example of this took place out of Churchill Falls in 1979 when cross-country skier, Gerry Kobelenko, left Churchill Falls to ski to Nain. There was an uneasy feeling about his ability to avoid getting lost among the local people like Max McLean, Dick Budgell and the late Stan Baikie. Baikie Lake, located just east of Ossokmanuan Lake is named after Stan.

Mr. Kobelenko set off for Nain, but a few days after his departure, strong winds and stormy weather arose. A couple of weeks passed, and still uneasy about the well-being of the man, Max and his friends convinced the RCMP to launch a search. The local men suggested to the police that they search the George River area as the believed the skier might traverse too far west and north. Sure enough, the police found the man in a fishing cabin on the George River. Max recounted the story to me recently and said the man was indeed way off course. He was also quite cold as he had not much heavy clothing. They brought him back to Churchill and helped him to regain his strength and gave him time to decide whether he wanted to continue. He wanted to make it to Nain and he set out again. About six weeks later, he arrived safely at Nain.

Labrador weather changes rapidly and what starts to be a warm, pleasant day can become cold and wet. Even in summer, layered clothing is best. Sweating should be avoided, as damp clothing doesn't provide much warmth when you need it. Avoid getting sweaty, as this will cause chilling when you stop moving. Try to have a complete change of clothes. Layering of clothes allows you to remove clothing when it gets too warm, but it's there to put back on when you cool down and need it.

When you are travelling by boat dress warmly as you will be standing around on deck and not moving much. You can get chilled pretty quickly. The Labrador Sea is icy-cold in summer, around 4°C – 5°C, so the hull of the boat will be cool. Your feet can get cold, so wear warm socks, a hat and gloves or mitts. Windproof clothing is very important and always wear – don't just carry or look at – a life jacket or Personal Floatation Device. If you don't have your own PFD, ask the boat operator where they are stored. Put one on!

Even in summer it is wise to wear a personal floatation vest, even if you are not in a boat. A sudden gust of wind causes a loss of balance while standing on a rock or bank and you could be in some turbulent water where the vest will be your friend.

SIXTEEN

Camp Stoves, Tents, Food and Water

Lightweight tents designed for backpacking should be carefully selected and bought from a reputable vendor as there are some products that just don't stand up to Labrador conditions, like high winds, heavy rains, and mists. Wind speeds of over 160 kilometres an hour have been recorded and there are sometimes few trees to break the wind. We know of instances where high winds have ripped through a certain kind of tent.

If you are carrying a camp stove using fuel other than wood, kerosene and naphtha are available at stores in Labrador communities. Again, stoves should be capable of operating in high winds and damp conditions. When you are travelling in Labrador it is wise to carry dried food like pitsik or nikkuk (dried fish and caribou) as it is lightweight and does not require cooking. Mixtures of dried fruit and nuts (be sensitive to any one in your party who has allergies) are also very good and provide nourishment because our cool environment and rugged terrain places demand on your body energy and reserves. There's plenty of water in Labrador but you should be cautious and use only running water or water from a reasonably sized pond or lake that is not stagnant.

Cooking meals over an open fire can be fun and very delicious, especially if you are fortunate to have your own chef. Here CBC Broadcaster Fred Armstrong starts the day with bacon and eggs! As Fred and others always say <u>Never</u> <u>Leave</u> <u>Camp</u> <u>Until</u> YOUR FIRE IS OUT - DEAD OUT.

By now you may be wondering how you are supposed to respond to the call of Mother Nature. In this day and age, you no doubt have some tissue with you. You use outdoors. Dig a pit into the snow and drop the pants. If there's a stiff breeze on, keep the bum to the wind so the pee doesn't spray back over you. Do the job and when you're finished, cover it over with the snow you just heaped up. If you are on the land and in summer, you can do the same thing and bury everything with soil or stones. Individual amounts of feces can also be left on the ground, away from trails, as the sunlight and air will speed up the decomposition. If you are travelling as a group you can use a communal area dug into about 15 – 20 cm and cover it over after each use. If you have toilet paper, minimize the amount used and burn it after. Tampons should be packed out with other garbage or burned. Tampons should never be buried.

Wastewater from washing and dish cleaning should not be dumped into ponds, lakes or streams. It is best to dispose of it in soil or sandy areas as then it can filter into the earth and break down before it reaches any bodies of water. Food scraps can be packed out when you leave; however, if you are attracting bears or other critters then burn it each day.

We can never go wrong by giving an extra word of caution about wind to workers and visitors new to the area. The winds and gusts around high elevations and across the land can be very powerful. These gusts can tip an adult off balance and can cause serious slips and falls, a dangerous element when near cliffs and up on the hills. A word of caution when taking photographs or using binoculars: Don't walk or move when using your equipment, as your focus and attention is reduced.

SEVENTEEN

Sharing Space with Other Critters

We don't have snakes or crocks, but there are some animals you should be aware of and give space to. Small and big game is quite plentiful in Labrador.

Small Animals

Porcupines are easy to kill, good eating, and serve as a table food, and can be counted on in times of emergency.

The small animals often seen crossing roads or which you may run into on your hike are porcupine, rabbit, fox, and squirrel. Although sighting and catch reports are scanty, wolverine and skunk have been taken. There was a skunk caught by trapper Henry Pottle near Rigolet in the 1940's. Mr. Pottle relayed the story to me in a CBC Radio interview in the mid-1970's and he said it had such a powerful odour that his dog team would not approach the pelt.

Wolverines

Wolverines are known as animals capable of destroying property and stealing cached food. The Innu even went as far as to design a death trap for the elusive scavenger. My father, Richard White, collected a sample of a special rig the Innu made for catching this animal. It was made of a long stick set at a 45-degree angle over a cluster of sharp pointed stakes set in the ground. A baited string was hung from the pole directly over the stakes. Mr. Wolverine climbs the stick, reaches for the bait, loses its balance and falls into the maze of sharp stakes and dies quickly of its injuries. My father, who set up his trading post at Voisey's Bay in 1913 also recorded buying wolverine skins in the winters of 1923, 1928, 1935 and 1937 from Inuit and Innu hunters and trappers.

Wolverines are still spotted occasionally in Labrador. I saw one in early May, 1970, in the vicinity of the giant waterfalls on the Churchill River, before the waterfalls were dried up through the diversion of the river. It crossed the road in front of me about a half-mile from the Brinco Bridge on the western side of the river. There is absolutely no doubt in my mind that it was a wolverine as I had seen and studied many pictures of the creature and ironically had just read a book on them about a week or so before this experience. Other sightings have been made in the Nain area along with quite a number of instances where the tracks of this elusive animal have been seen.

Like the wolverine, there are other animals that are quite discrete about where and when they make an appearance. They are the wolf, pine marten, ermine, beaver, muskrat, otter, and lynx. Up to now, there have been no known reports of coyotes.

Wolves

It is sometimes a real treat to encounter wolves, but these are very shy animals and avoid coming close to us. To hear them communicating in the early evening is a wonderful experience. In March 1997, I was at my old homestead near Nain, and Joey Angnatok was visiting from Nain. It was about 8:00 P.M., the stars were out, and the moon was rising for the night. There were a few caribou migrating through at the time.

Wolves like to hang out in the vicinity of caribou herds.

We were having a mug of tea and the evening was still and peaceful. Then we heard the distant call of a wolf. We stood outside the house and listened to the call coming from about a mile away to the east. Two or three minutes passed and another wolf answered the first call. It was about due south of our old house. Then Joey decided to place a call. He sent out two calls and then the wolf from the east responded and its curiosity grew as it came closer and closer to where we were. In about fifteen minutes, we could see on the moonlit harbour ice the outline of the big animal. It came to about 300 metres from us and then determined that we were authentic wolves. It turned and ambled off into the night. From then on the calls continued for a while and then stopped.

It is rare to see wolves in daylight unless you are an experienced hunter or unless they are sick with distemper or rabies and then they are uncharacteristically bold. If you should see a fox or wolf behave in a rabid manner, move away to avoid any contact. You should also report this to the provincial wildlife authorities or the RCMP. The Webb brothers in Nain, like Ron, Ches, and Joe are very experienced with wolves and other fur bearing animals in the area.

Moose and Caribou

Of the larger animals there are moose and caribou. Labrador is part-time home to the world's largest caribou herd, the George River herd that migrates between Quebec and Labrador. These graceful animals are the king of the animals for the Innu people and also the Inuit and Metis. Moose are relative newcomers to Labrador in large numbers, although my mother, who was born north of Nain in Nain Bay, told me that my grandfather, Renatus Hunter, once killed a moose with spear and bow and arrow when he was a young man in around 1880 in Nain Bay.

Two moose at Otter Creek in Happy Valley/Goose Bay. Moose and auto collisions are common on the island part of this province and there have been a couple of collisions on the road, route 520, to Northwest River and Shehatshiu.

Bears

Other big game you may encounter are the black bear and polar bear.

Over the past ten to fifteen years there are more and more adventurers, hikers, campers, and kayakers coming to Labrador, and especially to the region north of Nain. As a result, there are more encounters with polar and black bears. There have been half a dozen or so visitors who have killed polar bears claiming it was in self-defence. Many local people wonder whether it was actually necessary or just a case of being a trigger-happy visitor. In any case, polar and black bears can be dangerous. They are big, they are fast and they are powerful. In my opinion, they can go anywhere they like and do anything they want. Africa has it lions…we have our bears!

Bears are curious and inquisitive creatures. There are some things you can do to prevent problems. Be alert and watchful for signs of bears like paw prints or piles of bear dung. If you meet or see one stop, change your course and turn away from the animal. If you are in polar bear country, you should carry a firearm. Experienced Labrador hunters say a high-power rifle like a 30.06 or a 12-gauge pump action shotgun using rifled slugs is suitable protection. I like the 12-gauge idea as it also permits you to have shot shells in case you are caught out or lost without food.

Don't approach any bears for a photograph or other reasons. Parks Canada and the Alaskan wildlife people have outlined some good guides to follow. They say to always ensure your camp is clean and keep your food well covered. Burn your garbage and human waste frequently. Have a "second door" or escape route out of your tent in case there is a bear parked at your front door. Leslie Pardy of Cartwright told me that he was camped in a tent at Muddy Bay once and heard something outside his tent. He opened the door flap and met practically nose to nose with a black bear. He's not sure today who got the biggest fright.

Check around the landscape daily for any signs of bear, and each morning for any signs that a bear may have visited. Should you have to resort to a gun do it early. If a bear is around, I would waste no time in firing a few warning shots a few feet to the side of it. That will generally send them off.

Black bears are scroungers. They love fish and all kinds of food. They can walk right into a cabin and trash it just like humans who break into someone's home. I left an Old Town Tripper canoe at Harp Lake on a scaffold in 1990 and thought I had cleaned the smell of fish out of it. I guess there was a little trace somewhere and a bear mauled holes into that canoe and tore up the bottom. If you leave anything like food or garbage it is sure to attract them. Another bear stole my Arctic char pitsik during the night at my old homestead near Nain. The same bear got into our porch and stole a seal flipper that my son Jake and

This young lad in Postville proudly shows the bear his Inuit father harvested in 1999.

his cousin Matt had stored to take back to St. John's to show their friends. I stayed up several nights waiting for it to come around, but I never got the chance to fire one over him.

Bluff the Bear

Black bears can be trained. One of the best I've seen in recent times was when Bruce Gear of Hopedale was working at Shapio Lake Lodge. A trio of black bears committed a "break and enter" into the main lodge where Innu had stayed for a few weeks in the spring of 1991. When they left the lodge, they also left some garbage. The garbage attracted the three who broke in and ransacked the place. When they were finished, they had destroyed about $8,000.00 worth

Bears can be trained, but it is not recommended in Labrador. Bruce and Bluff.

of equipment and furnishings. When Bruce and his crew got settled in to clean up the damage, Bruce had to kill two of the huge, old bears, but he spared the younger follow. It got used to Bruce and the crew and they were kind to it. They treated it well and fed it. Bruce also trained it and named it Bluff.

Bluff followed them around the campsite, just like the family dog, as they did their chores. As time went on, the crew could feed it by hand and it listened to commands. Bruce and others even trained Bluff to be gentle to the point that they could pet it like a dog. They went ever further. Bruce could place a piece of food between his own teeth and Bluff, now face to face with Bruce, would gently and carefully take the protruding food from Bruce's mouth. I've never heard of this before, and probably will not see it again for a long, long time.

A Bear Avoided

D.J. (Don) Zieman of Newmarket, Ontario, and his friend Don Wales were north of Nain in August 2002 on a kayaking trip to Sudlek, also called Saglek. They hired Chesley Webb of Nain to take them a distance northward by longliner boat and were dropped off. They had two encounters with bears. A black bear tore up parts of their kayak buoyancy gear while they were hiking above the shore around the Kiglaipait Mountains. The bear took Don's firearm out of the kayak and carried it about twenty metres and then decided to drop it. Not much else happened there.

When Zieman and Wales were paddling around Rose Island they were in the vicinity of some shoals and spotted a polar bear swimming toward them, diving and then coming up closer to them. Zieman had talked things over with his Nain guides and he understood and valued the traditions and wishes of the people. He knew he should not kill a bear unless he absolutely had to so he began to make a kill prevention plan. He and Wales changed their course 180 degrees and paddled to a nearby rock and landed. The bear was still in the same curious mode and obviously intended to hang around them. Zieman took out his gun and aimed about ten to fifteen feet to one side of the white animal and pulled the trigger. His high-power rifle bullet struck the water and the report sent the bear off in the opposite direction. The two men changed their course away from the bear's vicinity and all parties continued to enjoy the awesome Labrador Sea.

The Parks people say that if a bear approaches, get on your snowmobile or in your car and drive away. If you must, drop a pack or item of clothing to divert the bear's attention. Shout, make noise, and defend yourself with whatever you can find.

Moses and the Polar Bear

Another encounter I can't help mentioning, although it didn't take place here in Labrador, was the encounter between an Inuit man and a polar bear in Nunavut. I was working with CBC North as a radio broadcaster out of Iqaluit at the time. In the summer of 1993, Moses Aliyak was camped with his wife and youngster at Corbett Bay in the Rankin Inlet region. The three family members were away from their tent when Mr. Aliyak heard his wife calling to him. He looked across the valley to see what was wrong and he spotted the problem. A polar bear was approaching his wife.

The rifle was back in the tent so Moses ran toward the polar bear and positioned himself between it and his wife. He tried to divert the bear but the big animal continued toward him. Moses knew his only option was to face the bear. At sixty-two, Moses was a small man, but in very good shape as he lived almost continuously on the land. The bear stood on its hind legs, and bear and man made contact. In lightning speed, Moses placed himself directly against the chest of the bear and both began wrestling. Moses managed to grip the bear's wrists, which prevented the bear from effectively clawing Moses.

For every move the bear made, Moses countered. When the bear tried to tear into Moses with its teeth, Moses placed his arm upright between the bear's jaws so the bear couldn't bite down. At that moment, Moses slightly crouched, with one arm holding the bear's wrist and the other in the bear's jaws; he manoeuvred his shoulder under the chest of the bear and gave a powerful heave. The force sent the bear backwards into the air and it landed on its back. It got up, shook itself and ran off. Moses was scratched up and had some gashes on his body, but did not have any serious injuries.

Seven years later, Moses Ailyak was camped in the same region again. Again another bear attacked the Inuit camp. An elderly woman, Hattie Amitnaaq, was killed. Two young boys were at the camp. One was seriously injured. Again Moses was without a firearm and stood up to the bear to protect his family. Moses wrestled the bear and again the bear left without further harming the campers. This time Moses was quite seriously injured and the surviving campers got him back to Rankin Inlet where he had to be airlifted to hospital in Winnipeg. In 1994, Moses Ailyak was given the Nunavut Award of Bravery by Nunavut Commissioner Peter Irniq for risking his life to save his family and companions. He was presented with the same award again in 2000 for his bravery in the second attack.

Birds

Labrador is on migration routes for many birds and in summer there are a lot that take up residence in the region. From the smallest songbirds to the hawks, owls, ducks, and geese as well as the eagles and ospreys, this is a bird watcher's haven. There are several very important gathering places along our coastline for eider ducks and the endangered harlequin duck can be spotted in the right habitat. The peregrine falcon spends its summer here and I have seen them or heard their unmistakable call quite a number of times in the past twenty years. I have enjoyed watching an immature American bald eagle perched on top of a spruce tree while I picked bakeapples on the land behind the old homestead near Nain. I have also had the great experience of having a pair of common loons display their dance across the water, and extraordinary flight to entice me away from their nesting young on the Unknown River. Storms and gales have also brought unusual birds to our communities.

There are some birds that stay in Labrador all year like the common raven, chickadee, sparrow, Canada jay or whiskey jack, ptarmigan and spruce grouse.

EIGHTEEN

Clothing and Camping

There are many books and good source material about camping and clothing. Cyril Goodyear, who lives in Deer Lake and is a former mayor of that town, spent most of his life in Labrador. He camps and does a lot of canoeing and lives an outdoor life. He has written a very good book about camping and survival, which you might want to get your hands on. It's called Nunatsuak. Another good source for tips and experience is a book by Horace Goudie of Happy Valley-Goose Bay called *Trails to Remember*.

A few tips I have picked up or learned from mistakes and would like to pass on includes a caution about what you are buying in footwear and clothing. While some of those hi-tech clothing designs are very attractive and fashionable, I'd like to give some advice and caution. I got one of those jackets that claim to stack up against mother nature. It's complete with woolen liner, and was handed on to me from my younger son, Jake, when his arms started coming down to about six inches below the cuff! Anyway, I had this fine jacket on in Davis Inlet last January when the wind was out of the west at forty miles per hour and the temperature was 28 below. As I stepped out into the wind, the jacket seemed to stiffen up. I noticed the material began to make a cracking sound. The jacket seemed to draw the cold. This was a $250.00 jacket and had I been on snowmobile or stranded out somewhere, it would not have been happy camping!

And do you know those rubber, knee-high green boots with the removable liner? Well, I must say they are pretty good, but here's a tip. I once tried on a pair of size eights with the liners in them. I had socks on and they felt just fine so off I went. After the first full day of use, I noticed that they had gotten bigger or my foot had gotten smaller … the boots had become too big. The weight of my foot had flattened the liners and the space inside the moulded boot got bigger. It was no longer a snug fit.

When buying a boot for a size-eight person, a size-seven boot and liner will do. After the liner has stretched and flattened with wear, it will provide the correct fit. People like Judy Saunders or Bruce Haynes at Northern Lights store in Happy Valley-Goose Bay know about this tidy bit of information so drop in to see them for properly fitting footwear.

I once tried to light a fire with a lighter and soon found myself with a useless lighter. I always carry wooden matches, and on long trips make sure I have waterproof ones. The little paper match booklets are fine close to home, but if you venturing more than a few miles, take the wooden ones. Getting a fire going in wet weather can be a real test. Old trappers and prospectors like John Michelin and Austin Montague had the proven know-how. It was John Michelin who guided many adventurers in the 1930's, '40's and '50's into the heartland of Labrador and back. If there are any birch trees around, the bark off the tree makes an excellent starter topped up with all the small dry branches you can find under and inside the limbs of spruce trees.

Labrador is wet with lots of bog, marsh, streams, and water everywhere. With all this wetland, it is important to travel with good boots that fit well. Some of those fancy hiking boots can be a bit of a pain as well so I recommend a good fitting rubber type like the Sorels and Kamik (kamik is the Inuit word for boot). Always tuck in an extra pair of socks and a pair of running shoes into your knapsack to give yourself a break when you get onto dry ground again.

When you are active, you don't need to wear a lot of heavy clothes. Save those to wear when you have stopped and are waiting around. Remove any clothes that cause you to sweat, because later, when you stop, the sweat will begin to freeze in your clothing. Certain types of rain gear can cause sweating inside, so carry a spare fleece jacket to replace any damp shirts.

In winter, the best clothing to wear, if you can get it made, is a pair of seal or caribou skin pants worn over woolen or cotton long johns or baggy woolen pants. The best footwear is made from sealskin for wet or dry travelling and from caribou hide for cold, dry snow conditions. These are worn over woolen duffel socks or several pairs of thick socks.

The jacket or parka with hood attached is made of caribou or sealskin and is at least three-quarter length down over the pants. The best mitts are again from seal or caribou lined with duffel wool or wrist-length mitts. Our mothers made all of this for us in times past, and some of the remaining professional seamstresses are still able to produce them. People like Minnie Merkeratsuk and Sarah Ittulak in Nain are among the best. For caribou clothing May Jane Nui, Agatha Piwas, or Marie Georgette Mistenapeo in Natuaushish are among the top producers this side of Nunavik. The key to all this clothing business, no matter what type, is that at the end of each day, turn everything inside out and hang it to dry, ready for the next day. This is real clothing!

Our weather can change from warm to cool to cold very rapidly. In the fall, it is best to wear wool and fleece jackets, good warm lined pants, or long johns. As we get into November it is time to dress with winter-type clothing. A good combination would be thermal johns under a pair of slacks or slacks covered by wind pants.

For other outerwear, a shirt over a sweater or fleece jacket and outside that a good, wind-resistant jacket preferably with a hood. A cap or toque is handy and a pair of ski-type gloves is a must. In footwear, thick socks, good running shoes, or hiking footwear that you can waterproof with silicone spray, or the felt-lined winter boot will see you comfortable in most normal situations. It is best to dress for warmth and comfort than for style and fashion.

Author working as a CBC Radio reporter near Iqaluit on Baffin Island and wearing Caribou jacket and mitts.

Some of the basic things I like to carry are a pocketknife, some fishing line or string, a small amount of first aids items, fly repellent to feed the bugs in summer and warm late fall days, and wooden matches. Bridgett Blake in Rigolet also says that a safety pin is a handy little item to have. Besides its normal purpose, Bridgett says it can be fashioned into a fishhook as well. It doesn't hurt to add a kettle, tea bags, coffee, milk powder, hot chocolate packets and some sweetener. Stop by a small, dancing stream or a nice lake setting, boil the kettle and enjoy the hot drink and the moment. Just make sure the fire is well out before you leave and take your garbage home. Simple, uncomplicated, and refreshing

NINETEEN

Summary

The sun dips below the horizon casting its glow across the gentle swells of the Labrador coast.

I hope you have found this little book helpful. It is not intended to be a safety manual or replace any other material on travel in Labrador. Nor is it intended to portray Labrador as a dangerous place. Like any other region on our earth it has its dangers, but you can enjoy our great outdoors and land when you respect yourself, our land, and our people. The intent of this guide is to help you to enjoy your stay here, get back to your home satisfied and contented with your visit.

Labrador is awesome! The Big Land, is a land sitting on the edge of your own province or country. It is a land to discover, a place you cannot visit without being forever changed. A helicopter pilot friend of mine, John Danby, once showed me a sign he stuck on his map case. He told me he got it in Makkovik and it read "Visit Labrador. You'll Never Be The Same." I don't know who created that saying but whoever you are, you're right on!

Photo by Leroy Metcalfe.

Suggested Reading

Them Days magazines

Our Footprints Are Everywhere – Inuit Land Use

Innu Women Write

Trails to Remember – Horace Goudie

Daughter of Labrador – Millicent Loder

Labrador By Choice – Ben Powell

Woman of Labrador – Elizabeth Goudie

Green Trees, Blue Waters – Harry Paddon

Labrador Doctor – Tony Paddon

Labrador Inuit Legends – William F. Peacock

Nunatsiaak – Labrador the Big Land – Cyril Goodyear

Memories of My Childhood – Josephine Kalleo

Memories of My Life – Paulus Maggo

The Labradorians – Lynn Fitzhugh

Experience West Labrador

White Eskimo – Harold Horwood

Images of Labrador

A Labrador panorama.

Labrador Winter Games Dogteam winners, Goose Bay, 2003.

Boulder on an island west of Nain. Summer 1999.

Innu tent along the Northwest River road, Spring 1976.

Stay well away from polar bears.

Northwest River highway.